Tumults in Thinking

A Basic History of Western Philosophy from

Pre-Socratics to Postmodernists

Larry D. Harwood

Kendall Hunt
publishing company

Cover photograph © Samantha Oliva

publishing company

www.kendallhunt.com
Send all inquiries to:
4050 Westmark Drive
Dubuque, IA 52004-1840

For Thomas Augustine and Silvia Elizabeth

"Histories make men wise; poets witty; the mathematics subtle; natural philosophy deep; moral grave; logic and rhetoric able to contend."

Francis Bacon

Contents

Preface

The aim of these few pages is to present the history of philosophy in a concise manner and without the lengthy amplifications available in longer texts. The book presents a broad overview of philosophy, while providing significant details to indicate the complexity and rigor of the discipline through times of historical tumult, both in the emerging and eclipsing of ideas. As the book is not intended as an intensive or exhaustive history of the subject, major transitions in thinking and notable debates are highlighted. The book is largely but not exclusively intended for relative newcomers to philosophy; the text explicates philosophical positions for understanding philosophy through consideration of its broader history. While the beginner needs an overview of the historical landscape of philosophy, most do not need an encyclopedic volume providing infinite detail on the history of the subject. Thus, the brevity of this book on such a large subject is without apology.

Included are references to historical world events of seismic importance, such as the fall of the Roman Empire and the world wars of the twentieth century—these and other events with some influence upon and therefore of importance to the history of philosophy. Demarcations of the history of philosophy are present in the chapter headings and subheadings. Initial introduction to the history of the subject comes in a first chapter positioning philosophy by considering something of the past culture in which Western philosophy first arose. The last chapter concludes by asking whether the present postmodern culture of the West leaves any space for philosophy. The chapters in between chronicle the history of Western philosophy with focus on times of transition that changed philosophy.

Virtually no touted 'short' books on the history of philosophy are indeed short.[1]

The present book by contrast presents a summary view of the history of philosophy with due acknowledgment that there are larger texts of hundreds of pages that convey more information. For many classrooms, however, a much briefer text is required to prevent the reader from likely abandoning a tome fretfully weightier than the reader's dinner. Thus, the idea of this book is to present a short text on the long history of philosophy in the West. Such a text proved difficult to write, requiring the restraint to forego longer explications to which university teachers, myself included, are by nature habitually prone. Nevertheless, in short compass the book attempts to broadly organize the depths and tumults of philosophy into manageable form. By presenting a brief history of philosophy the student becomes acquainted with some of the contours of a subject often presented with too much or virtually no historical background.

Larry D. Harwood
Philosophy and History
Viterbo University
La Crosse, Wisconsin
October 2017

---

[1] For example, consider Nigel Warburton's *A Little History of Philosophy*, Yale University Press, 2011, in at 252 pages; or Anthony Kenny's *A Brief History of Western Philosophy*, Wiley-Blackwell, 1988, in at 365 pages; or Johannes Hirschberger's *A Short History of Western Philosophy*, Lutterworth Press, 2nd edition, 2008, in at 264 pages; or Robert Solomon and Kathleen Higgins's *A Short History of Philosophy*, Oxford University Press, 1996, in at 329 pages. Thomas Nagel's *What Does It all Mean? A Very Short Introduction to Philosophy*, Oxford University Press, 1987, is indeed short with only 101 pages, but contains not a single mention of any historical philosopher.

Acknowledgments

My students at Viterbo University are significantly responsible for the impetus of this book, both in form and content. Their pointed questions over what philosophy does and where philosophy comes from has aided me at crucial points in the writing of this text. For both professional and personal encouragement, I wish to thank a number of my university colleagues. To Dr. Glena Temple, my previous Dean at Viterbo University and now President of Viterbo, I am exceedingly grateful for constant unwavering and always assured support for my writing projects. To my current Dean, Dr. Tim Schorr, I am indebted for steady support of my work and his frequent encouragements. To my former department head, Dr. Bill Reese, I owe hearty thanks for discussions and conversations with him over the past years and for a friendship solidified through two decades of teaching many of the same students and some of the same subjects. To my current department head, Dr. Andrew Hamilton, I am appreciative for welcoming the imposition of philosophy and philosophers into the History Department at Viterbo. Partly from his example of peppering his history courses with relevant philosophical influences, I have increasingly chocked my philosophy courses with relevant historical background. To my wife Dottie, I owe plentiful thanks for always giving ear to my fascination with the history of thinking and the thinkers and times behind the thinking. Furthermore, heartfelt thanks are due to her for unflinching support of this project and her often needed encouragements. Lastly, I am indebted to the great philosopher Ludwig Wittgenstein for his suggestion that the purpose of philosophy is "to show the fly the way out of the fly-bottle." My purpose in a prior book was to show the reader how the fly got into the bottle in the beginning.[1] My main concern in this book is to provide some history of the fly's flight while in the bottle.

---

[1] Harwood, *Putting Philosophy in Its Place: A Preface to the Life of Philosophy*, Kendall Hunt, 2014.

Introduction: Philosophy and Mythology in the Ancient World

In our day it is commonplace to think of philosophy as provoking a radical and novel form of thinking necessarily antagonistic toward the customs of the day. However much such an impression might be exaggerated, though at times true in much of the history of the Western world, it seems less so in the East. In Hinduism and Buddhism, for example, a Western reader is rather immediately struck by how philosophically orientated and astute are some of the texts of these traditions. One might object, however, that what we find in these cases, though admittedly evidence of some philosophical finesse, is hardly the kind of interrogation that qualifies as philosophy. In response to that objection, however, we might counter that the objector simply proves the point. That is, the proclivity of Western philosophy is to assume that philosophy is by nature adversarial, the voicing of a disagreement or dissent. It is scarcely cause for wonder, then, that when the observer looks for contentiousness—if that is what philosophy is—he finds philosophy.

Leaving the extent of the combativeness of philosophy and philosophers aside for the moment, it is true that in the Western world philosophers begin to partially set aside some mythological traditions imbedded in their cultures. However, such changes usually require some time before producing significant turns within culture: the changes very rarely create seismic reverberations at precisely the time of introduction. Most often there is an ebb and flow of ideas even among philosophers, but rarely does one philosophical house come down instantaneously for the benefit of an immediate successor. There are normally steps leading up to such changes. Tumults of a sort may churn the intellectual waters into something of a new configuration. Very

1

infrequently is the direction of the waters revamped entirely, though the early Greek thinkers seem to provide something of an example of a rather radical turn in thinking.

The emerging tendency among some early Greek philosophers to rethink the standard ways of thinking and explanation did not typically carry with them fiery rebellion denouncing existing myths. These new thinkers might be dismissive toward the myths, but usually such myths were simply set aside for the sake of alternative account, without robust mocking of the traditional account. In another estimation, the originality of new thinking might be seen as something of a marvel, however aloof from the world of practicalities the thinking of the philosopher might be. That is, the innovations of philosophy might set aside some existing ways of thinking, but perhaps without a direct or protracted confrontation, such as we are somewhat familiar with in modern and contemporary culture where ideologies are often glaringly poised in overt opposition. Thus, the controversy aroused by Charles Darwin's theory of evolution in the nineteenth century certainly registered more animosities than Plato's charge that much of what Homer and Hesiod said or implied about the Greek gods was untrue.

Nonetheless, the change of ideas in a culture moving from Greek mythology to Greek rationalism was stark, even if such a change was hardly realized by the mass of humans living within that culture. In other words, truth be told, the transition from the stories of Homer to the dialogues of Plato is hardly anything less than colossal, because conceptions of the world are drastically different. As explanations for how the world works and something of the human relation to the world the two are in notable contrast. Any reader of today perusing Plato and Homer's writings can feel the difference.

However, it is pertinent to consider that except for the innovators and people keenly perceptive toward ideas and changes in ideas, most people in the short duration of a human lifetime—particularly a normally short one compared to our relative longevity today—would scarcely have noticed such a shift. The same could be likened to the much later discoveries of the Scientific Revolution of the seventeenth century. That is, the ordinary citizen at the time of early modernity would scarcely have reason to notice the new understanding of how the world worked conceived by a Galileo or a Newton. Any such awareness would have to wait until the later Industrial Revolution concretized some of that new understanding of an old world with material inventions in the new. When novel innovations came into the home or workplace or onto the battlefield they came without much need of introduction: the products of new thinking and invention could be visually witnessed as vastly altering the conditions of material life. This impression would be conveyed to an observer whether that observer was literate or illiterate. Advances in the use of medicine and the harnessing of steam for power, as further examples, served to demonstrate to virtually everyone that material changes were remaking their world. Perhaps most importantly to these human witnesses, they might be able to live something of a better or longer life because of these new innovations.

The philosophers, however, while producing new or revised conceptions of the world, did not aim at producing material objects or necessarily making material life more bearable or increasing human longevity in that world. For such reasons, the philosopher quite naturally could be perceived as, and likely was, more of an oddity than an iconoclast. The iconoclast could be deliberately disruptive and even destructive, whereas the philosopher was simply and maybe even naively distinctly different from most other people. The philosopher was generally animated by a curiosity probably exceeding that of his peers. This was usually enough to attract attention to his person. Perhaps somewhat like today, philosophers might be thought of as thoughtful idlers, living in their mental worlds with scant notice of any of the rest of us, while probably everybody noticed him. In this way the philosopher could be as innovative or creative as the material inventor, but the philosopher was viewed as more concerned with things that did not concern, because they did not seem to affect, the common man. To this day, an appetite for philosophy and a fund of common sense seem often quite opposite in people; most satire lodged against philosophers exploits the presumed common knowledge present in nearly everyone except the aloof philosopher. Moreover, the differences between the two types of people also mean they are only rarely comfortable with one another, aware that to some degree each lives in a world to be contrasted to the world of the other.

This significant difference between others compared to the philosopher, however, still indicates little of what the philosopher does or that for which the philosopher hopes. Though usually befuddled by the philosopher, the common man would be understandably grateful to the material inventor for a labor-saving device, for example. However, the relationship between the philosopher and the ordinary man of virtually any historical period seems to reveal little of any relationship like this between the two. (This is why the philosopher is sometimes thought of as an elitist or even arrogant.) Part of the ravine here is because in philosophy any "solutions" or answers to problems—rare as such notoriously are in philosophy—probably find little or no immediate pedestal in a home or battlefield or workplace. That is, the common man tends to see little of obvious or tactile value in the work of the philosopher. This is because the questions of philosophy seem far afield from the affairs of the life of the common man. The philosopher, seen in this light, might truly be a genius, but also worthless, and given even time, perhaps a great nuisance to his community.

Perceived primarily as odd and something of a nuisance, the future for a philosopher might not seem to hold much promise. In Ancient Greece, however, particularly in Athens, while the philosopher might not be welcomed, he might be tolerated, even if mocked and sometimes considered something of a buffoon. This was because in Athens democracy was in a fledgling infancy and opinions and oftentimes contentious opinions could be voiced. However, the beginnings of philosophy in Greece also put the rumblings of philosophers in proximity to and thus in notable contrast to the inherited traditional myths of that culture. It is certainly plausible to conjecture that those beholden to the traditional myths could have experienced at least something of an initial conflict not to say collision with the philosophers. The enterprise of philosophy (and science) aims to overcome ignorance with knowledge on the presumption that the latter is preferable to the former. Philosophers historically have expended great efforts in trying to figure something out that has not been figured out previously. Often they try to improve upon, or totally revise a previous explanation deemed faulty at points or perhaps totally fallacious. Philosophers acting out of such motivations are not surprisingly going to create at least some stir in their communities.

For philosophers who might have suggested that the Greek myths were not serious nor believable cosmologies, trouble was a distinct possibility. However, partially mitigating any such conflict in the case of ancient Greece, for example, was the fact that there was no established order of priests who could have constituted a front line of resistance or even attack on philosophers. It is pertinent to note here, moreover, that the first Western martyr of philosophy, Socrates, died at the hands of Athenian jurors who did charge him with something of a religious (and political) crime of deflecting due allegiance to the Greek gods (and the Greek city-state of Athens). In other words, some differing allegiances are certainly evident in the struggle between Socrates and his accusers. All the same, in Athens at the time some democratic feeling provided some license to the philosopher to voice his views—at least to a point.

However, the separation of myth or custom from philosophy is very rarely cleanly or absolutely separated as will be observed in the Pre-Socratic philosophers. Moreover, it can be seen in both Socrates and Plato. Starting with the Pre-Socratics, we witness thinkers who preserve vestiges of older mythological traditions alongside their novel attempts to reason out for greater human understanding the structures of the world. For example, a full picture of Socrates and his teaching discloses a man genuinely believing himself a man sent by deity (of some sort) to awaken the Athenians out of their slumbers and ignorance. In this role he might be seen as much a prophet or seer as a philosopher. The impression Socrates made upon his contemporaries and what impression he makes upon us should be distinguished when different, if we are to perceive somewhat correctly Socrates and his times.

Chapter 1
Ancient Philosophy

1. A. Pre-Socratic Philosophy

Ancient philosophy in the Western world begins in Greece with a group of thinkers collectively referred to as the Pre-Socratics. Pre-Socratics as a designation refers to those philosophers historically prior to Socrates, beginning with Thales (624– 546 BC), notable for his view that "all is water." These thinkers, about which we generally know very little, attempted to answer the question, "what is reality?" With this question, they would be initiating a question of metaphysics, but with some of the answers given, they read like primitive scientists of a sort. Indeed, the distinction between science and philosophy is not yet clear at this time.

What is most significant about these thinkers is that they are beginning to displace the mythological view of the world inherited from Greek mythology with a rational look at the world. "Rational" means in some sense naturalistically, without reference to the gods or supernatural explanation, but the transition is better understood as the search for the principles of order within nature over the sporadic and causal activity of supernatural entities. The works of Homer reveal an unpredictable world for the most part, except for the fact that Homer presumes there are boundaries of a sort that even the gods do not dare provoke. The gods nevertheless script what happens in nature while holding humans to some degree accountable for their actions. The gods are not notably moral themselves, a fact that Plato will later note as a reason to distrust the Greek poet's understanding of deity. The world of Greek mythology is a world in which virtually anything can happen; the world of Greek philosophy is a world in which reason attempts to understand what does happen.

Hippocrates (c. 460– c. 370 BC) is a good example of this shift, even though he is not

technically a philosopher per se, but rather often referred to as the father of medicine.

Hippocrates attempts to understand what in his day was called the "sacred disease" that we now

know as epilepsy. Hippocrates diagnosed the phenomena in terms of physiology and

psychology, rather than as a visitation of the gods. Other questioners probing for knowledge

looked for coherence and symmetry as a key, causing some philosophers, like the Pythagoreans

(origins in the sixth century BC), to surmise that reality was structured mathematically. But

whether the answer was mathematics or matter, the quest was for something that could explain

reality on the basis of some rational principle of determinacy or order.

Thales is usually credited with being the first Western philosopher, but this means that he

is the first one we find referred to in later writings of other philosophers. No writings of his

survive. Thales was interested in the question of what is the ultimate stuff of the universe, as

were the other Pre-Socratic philosophers, and his answer was water. He purportedly also said

that "all things are full of gods," but the explanation of water and not gods signaled a new kind

of explanation of things. Very few thinkers make a completely clean break with the past, though

Thales probably reflects with his reference to the gods a search for the dynamism in nature.

Thales had not picked water as a random answer to the core stuff of the universe, but as

remarked by Aristotle, he probably observed the frequency with which moisture accompanied

nature, and postulated that all diverse phenomenon were therefore derivative from a single

source.

Thales's successors were Anaximander (c. 610– c. 546 BC), a contemporary pupil of

Thales, and Anaximenes (c. 585– 528 BC). They continued with the same question of Thales,

but Anaximander did not postulate a single specific thing or element, like water as the source of

all

things, but rather, advanced the notion that all things derive from an indefinite and boundless realm. While this answer may sound mystical, Anaximander's intent seems to be for an entity that was itself not determinate, but rather the source of all determinate things. His search seems to be for an infinite primordial source that can explain the finite variety of determinate things. He seems particularly interested in the process of beginnings, both cosmological and biological, and makes the astounding observation for his day that the human species must have begun as another species since the human is extraordinarily helpless in infancy.

Anaximenes, as a younger contemporary of Anaximander, posited air as the ultimate stuff of reality. This answer may appear to regress to the limitation of a specific entity, as with Thales's answer, but Anaximenes thought the answer of a boundless entity too vague, without however rejecting the intention of Anaximander. Anaximenes, therefore, conceived of air as the boundless. Air is everywhere he figured, and different configurations of air account for the different things we observe. He made reference to rarefaction and condensation as processes of the motion of air giving rise to different things, and further stipulated that qualitative differences among objects is due to quantitative differences.

These three thinkers make no distinction between the material and immaterial world, and to us appear to be materialists, though they formulate no explicit argument that matter is the origin and basis of all reality. In a sense they are materialists without knowing it. Other thinkers of this time, however, will attempt to explain the stuff of reality by reference to entities that are not themselves material. Here too, we will encounter the first philosophical school where religion will be interfaced with philosophical thinking.

The Pythagoreans, who take their name from Pythagoras (c. 490– 421 BC) postulated that numbers were the basis of all things. Pythagoras left the island of Samos for southern Italy and settled in the Greek city of Crotone, and it is he who discovered that the square of thehypotenuse of a right-angled triangle is equal to the squares of the other two sides—hence, the Pythagorean Theorem. The Pythagoreans noticed that the form of reality corresponded to mathematical proportions and the like, and therefore for them matter was not ultimate but rather the structure or form of reality. This notion would not be unlike that which we find in modern science where the gravitational pull of the earth can be described mathematically.

Beyond these metaphysical notions about reality the Pythagoreans were mathematicians/philosophers for another reason. For them, philosophy and mathematics were conducive to a certain kind of life, and not merely subject matter that one idly learned. The Pythagoreans had interest in purifying the soul and thus gave attention to what could produce purification of the soul. They made a place for music in their studies and regarded it as therapeutic for the soul. Noting that the intervals between musical notes could be exhibited mathematically seemed to give credibility to their notion of the pervasiveness of mathematical symmetry in the world. They thought that by lifting one's attention to things that in a sense were above the earth—like theory, like mathematics, like music—one could purge one's soul. Some of these notions would have tremendous influence upon Plato.

Though Thales, Anaximander, Anaximenes, and the Pythagoreans were looking for the real or permanent stuff of the universe, what made any answer to that question difficult was the observation that things change from one thing to another. While these thinkers had tried to address what that thing was, whether material—or immaterial, as with the Pythagoreans—other Pre-Socratic philosophers will concentrate upon analyzing change itself. Heraclitus (c. 530-470 BC) claimed that all things were in a state of flux. Therefore change itself was the only permanent feature of reality. He contended that one cannot step twice into the same river because the movement of the water prohibits this action from occurring. Therefore permanence is revealed, but paradoxically what is revealed is the impermanence of all things. However, Heraclitus did not think of change as corresponding with the capriciousness of the gods of Greek mythology. Rather, constant change is a function of an eternal Reason or Logos which permeates all things. Furthermore, Heraclitus thinks that this constant change is decipherable in terms of the laws of motion and change. Thus, there is a coherence to reality, despite the fact of constant fluctuation.

Parmenides (active around 500 BC) and a younger contemporary of Heraclitus, goes to the core of Heraclitus's philosophy by denying that there is any such thing as change. In the history of philosophy there are thinkers who have maintained ideas which seem at complete variance with common sense, but Parmenides reflects a basic belief of many philosophers that philosophy need not be governed by the parameters or the prison of common sense. Thus, oddity or presumably odd positions are a not infrequent feature of philosophical thinking. On the other hand, like other philosophers, Parmenides appealed to reason in his justification for claiming the truth of what seems an odd idea initially. Parmenides did not deny that there is an appearance of change in things, but he does deny that appearance is the same thing as reality. Furthermore, he claims that our senses are often the source of the opinion that something changes, but Parmenides asserts that the mind and reason must police what the senses mistake as real. This distinction will become crucial in Plato's philosophy.

A further development in ancient philosophy occurs about this time in the philosophy of Anaxagoras (500-428 BC). Whereas the distinction between the material and immaterial world is in evidence in the Pythagoreans, Anaxagoras further distinguishes between mind and matter. He contends that it is mind, or *nous*, that orders the arrangement of matter. Nevertheless,

Anaxagoras does not separate mind from matter as two interdependent things, because the two are for him always found together. Despite his introduction of mind or *nous*, Anaxagoras is criticized by both Plato and Aristotle for a lack of specificity about how mind works with and upon matter. This problem of how the two interact will be an issue discussed by many future philosophers up to the present day.

When we come to the philosophy of Leucippus and Democritus we confront a metaphysical theory which sounds extraordinarily modern, though Leucippus lived about 490-430 BC and Democritus, 460-360 BC. These philosophers conceived of reality as mechanical and materialistic. Reality is composed of only space, which is like a vacuum, and atoms. Everything that is, is a result of colliding atoms in this vacuum. Difference is accounted for in the collisions of atoms which join themselves to other atoms to produce differentiated products as unique as snowflakes. These thinkers made no recourse to God or nous as an ultimate explanation, for the void and the atoms are eternal and thus apparently suffice for satisfactory explanation.

Democritus ventured beyond the question of what is real to speak to epistemology and ethics. Though he was a materialist, Democritus distinguished between the perceptions of the senses and the mind and awarded greater reliability to the mind. Ultimately Democritus seemed to think that the mind offers objective knowledge that is compromised by the senses. In matters of ethics, Democritus urged moderation in all things, while contending that cheerfulness was the goal of life. These prescriptions, however, would seem to some later thinkers at variance with the implied determinism in Democritus' materialism.

Democritus' ethical interests were indicative of the future of philosophy for the focus of philosophy shifted about the time of Socrates (469-399 BC). The general reason given is that because the answer given to the question of the prior thinkers was answered in so many different ways, it appeared as possibly irresolvable and so philosophy moved on to other questions where answers might seem more promising. For these reasons, Socrates and Plato are hugely interested in humans, and particularly in ethics. However, Socrates, Plato, and Aristotle come on the heels of almost two centuries of philosophical thinking. Many of the philosophical positions of these three giants are thus partly articulated out of awareness of positions held by prior thinkers. Aristotle in particular in his writings pays notable historical attention to positions of his predecessors, and in the process informs us of much of the history of philosophy prior to him. He, like many philosophers after him, will see his own positions as largely improvements upon the positions of his predecessors.

1. B. Socrates

Socrates (469– 399 BC), though revered across the ages by subsequent philosophers, conducted his philosophical exercises and inquiries almost entirely in the streets and meeting places around Athens. This man was a notable feature of the Athenian scene for roughly a half century, but despite his notoriety and his later venerated place in the history of philosophy, to our knowledge Socrates himself wrote nothing. (This is a notable fact that is not that uncommon: neither did, so far as we know, Jesus or Siddhartha Gautama or Confucius write anything.) Nevertheless, despite this absence of writing by his own hand, we know quite a bit about him. There is some detail about the life and ideas of Socrates most notably in the writings of Plato, his student, but also in other contemporaries, such as Xenophon, an historian and philosopher of sorts, and Aristophanes, a playwright. Five of Plato's dialogues are called the Socratic dialogues, because in them Socrates is the main character. In these dialogues, such as the

Apology, we hear Socrates's defense of himself before his Athenian accusers, which results finally in his death sentence. Philosophically, Socrates's (and so too Plato's) interests are not those of the Pre-Socratics. Socrates is concerned with the human world, not the world of the cosmos or, for that matter, the matter of the material world. (Aristotle will be interested in that world, in contrast to both Socrates and Plato.)

Socrates had made some inquiry into what the pioneering Pre-Socratics had thought, but in the case of Anaxagoras, Socrates's initial enthusiasm met with bitter disappointment. When Socrates found reference in Anaxagoras to mind or *Nous* as a possible way to explain reality, he anxiously read on but found no further particulars. With Anaxagoras not expanding on this inviting idea, Socrates, annoyed, and perhaps a bit embittered, set his sights elsewhere. In such a fashion, Socrates would apparently decide that knowledge of the human world rather than cosmological explication was within reach of the philosopher's reason. Socrates, however, was not just abstractly concerned with what the human turned out to be as a result of study. That is, for Socrates the human person had a requirement laid upon his person, inasmuch as "the unexamined life is not worth living," as he famously contended at his trial. Philosophical inquiry had real purpose existentially for Socrates.

That Socrates could be and was executed in his locality of Athens points to the fact that he was not always popular or loved in Athens, despite his posthumous fame. Aristophanes, though providing some valuable details about Socrates in *The Clouds*, at the same time parodies Socrates's manner of inquisitive reasoning among the Athenians and makes of him something of a comic figure that many could hardly take seriously. Annoyance was probably a frequent estimation of the man. Socrates, however, was not one to be ruffled by public or other opinion. He apparently quite easily and almost effortlessly courted disagreement and opposition with an unbelievable calmness that would tax most ordinary mortals. Socrates especially rankled the

governing powers of Athens during the convulsion of the Peloponnesian War that was

devastating to Athens's previous eminence in the world. After the surrender to Sparta he is

placed on trial. Here too, he indifferently mocks his accusers, while refusing to compromise his

principles for the sake of his life. Not only are his accusers dismayed and angered over such a

stance, but his grieving friends are astounded by his unwaffling courage. Some of them may

have been tempted to regard him as possessing a bit of reckless foolhardiness.

Socrates presented an odd presence in his day (and probably for most any day in most

cultures) in part because he had an unwavering vision that dictated a mission to his

contemporaries that pushed most everything else to the periphery. Plato says that since a child,

Socrates had experienced an inner voice and Socrates could be found on occasion standing in the

same position for a twenty-four-hour period. He appears sometimes with something of the

temperament of a mystic, except that his keen insistence upon the demands of reason seems more

definitive for the man. In his philosophical volleys with his fellow citizens, he is relentless in the

pursuit of truth and knowledge, but because of it he probably appeared conceited to some.

Nevertheless, the impression of conceit is not evidenced in Socrates's desire to make

sense of the assertion of the Delphic Oracle that there was none wiser than Socrates. Such an

utterance from the Oracle about Socrates came to his notice through a friend who had recently

visited the Temple of Apollo at Delphi. In time, Socrates, who was initially befuddled by such

an honorific statement, came eventually to see that any superlative wisdom of his simply

consisted in his own realization and self-admission of his own ignorance, when he was in fact

ignorant. This realization of the true meaning of the oracle had taken a while, however, and led

Socrates to some of the purported wisest men among the Athenians. With them he discovered an unwillingness on the part of most to admit ignorance when they were caught with their ignorance showing despite their angry protests to the contrary. Socrates's dialogue with such persons certainly contributed something to a reserve of unpopularity, culminating in his trial. The spectacle of Socrates's unflattering castigations of pretenders, however, probably greatly amused some bystanders who surely reveled in such entertainment.

Socrates's conversations with others, particularly his young students, followed a set form, which is known as dialectic. In this dialectic someone proposes a solution to a problem, or the problem can take the form of a desired definition of something, such as knowledge, or virtue, or piety. The object of dialectic is to turn the proposed solution or definition every conceivable direction to examine its claim to cogency, and to squeeze out any contradictions or anomalies lurking behind it. In the exchange of dialectic, Socrates appears as the relentless philosopher who will accept no proposals that have not survived scrupulous questioning. Furthermore, many of these forays into dialectic terminate inconclusively simply because virtually no proposal or answer survives such unflinching scrutiny. Though this may be disappointing, Socrates is nevertheless unwilling to grant a deficient proposal a positive verdict simply for the sake of coming to a conclusion. Just as Socrates has the notion that the unexamined life is not worth living, so too he believes that one must attach oneself to ideas and ideals that have unfailingly passed the tests of truth. The interrogations of Socrates with his dialectic method and the meager results point to the fact that philosophy is a hard and sometimes apparently an unrewarding business. That is, the philosopher is rarely rewarded with his desired unequivocal answer to the posed question. Rather than an answer served on a silver platter, the philosopher's plight is one more akin to fighting tooth and nail for a goal most often seeming to resist one's very best efforts. Philosophy will therefore require patience and more than an afternoon conversation to get anywhere in the fray of positions disputed. For Socrates this is not too much to ask.

Socrates's desire for true definitions naturally leads to the content of his own philosophical ideas, and raises the whole question of whether the notions he articulates in Plato's Socratic Dialogues are really his ideas, or simply those of Plato. This is particularly the case since we have no writings of comparison from Socrates's hand. Nevertheless, most scholars are of the view that there is a blend of both thinkers in what Socrates is given to say. Nevertheless, it is virtually impossible to precisely distinguish Socrates's views from those of his pupil and chief chronicler, Plato.

What Socrates most wanted with a definition was to get at the essence of what the thing was or what fundamentally constituted the notion under consideration. In his dialectic, oftentimes someone would offer an example of the thing to be defined, like virtue or knowledge. An example of one possessing virtue, however, is not to define what virtue is, so as a definition an example will not do. Behind this difficulty in arriving at a definition is Socrates's notion that to get to the real thing one must go beyond or behind the individual things which merely exhibit or are an instance of the real thing. Furthermore, there seems a certain independence of say virtue from things that possess virtue, or even beauty from things that are beautiful. This notion will receive further treatment by Plato, and maintenance by way of revision in Aristotle's philosophy.

Socrates's moral philosophy has already been mentioned as something of a result of a turn from the cosmological speculations of many of the Pre-Socratics. However, as Democritus had spoken to issues of moral philosophy before him, Socrates found that he could not fashion his moral philosophy without interaction with competing moral philosophies in his day. Socrates encounters as the most uncongenial of the philosophers of his day the Sophists, who were relativists in ethics. This means that for them, there is no single or objective right or wrong. Rather, the morals one has derive from what community one belongs to, and communities of course have different conceptions. For Socrates this notion was pernicious, and indeed placed persons in charge of morals rather than morals being in charge of persons. That is, Socrates was an objectivist in ethics; right was right and wrong was wrong wherever one stood in Greece or no matter what years one lived. The Sophists, Socrates might have said, were simply too lazy to labor at the hard work of philosophy. Socrates never intimates that philosophy is easy, though it is rewarding, because in doing it, one is engaged in building or building up one's person in the way of wisdom.

As indicated, of all of his intellectual enemies the Sophists represented the most despised by Socrates, and two famous Sophists with which Socrates did battle were Protagoras (c. 490– c. 420 BC) and Thrasymachus (Fourth-century BC). Of these two Sophists, Protagoras is the better known, in part for his infamous humanistic statement that "man is the measure of all things." In a sense Protagoras looks upon human knowledge as constrained by the human faculty of knowing. This means that the human subject places a limitation upon what can be objectively known by that inquiring subject. Furthermore, Protagoras seemed to think that there is no common structure for knowing among people that would guarantee even a modicum of agreement among them. When he turns to ethics the same skepticism is evidenced in his denial that there is an objective morality. In light of the difference of moral opinion among cultures, what people should do is to give allegiance to the moral climate or culture in which they find themselves. This conclusion of Protagoras is noticeably at variance with the habitual philosopher who resists acceptance of custom. What makes Protagoras and the Sophists so intractable is that their appeal, like that of Socrates, partakes of reason.

Thrasymachus appears as a Sophist who might otherwise appear in his thinking to be merely a political despot in search of raw power. As indication of that, Thrasymachus contends that "right," as a moral term, simply stands for those who have the most power. From there is only a short waltz to "might makes right." This particular view, and the views of Protagoras made Sophists most loathsome to Socrates. Socrates holds that truth is the measure of all things and that the life that Protagoras suggests living is not worthy of the philosopher. As Socrates did not mince words with his intellectual combatants such as the Sophists, he can appear in the discussions recorded in Plato's dialogues to be sometimes downright belligerent and even mocking in debate. Undoubtedly, this kind of comportment, while drawing attention to the fearlessness of Socrates, also made him suspicious and troublesome to others. Decades of debate with him by Athenians probably produced not a few enemies but also powerful ones, which goes some way in explaining his demise.

1.C. *Plato*

Plato (c. 429– 347 BC)was sickened by the execution of his teacher Socrates and however little sympathy he might unlikely have had for the modicum of democratic rule of Athens, he had none at all after this act of unforgivable treachery. For Plato this atrocious act plainly evidenced the inability of people with wrong principles and vindictiveness to rule anybody and perhaps even themselves. Therefore, Plato's own undemocratic political philosophy makes notable place for philosophers groomed as "philosopher-kings" after an appropriate and extensive education. This is needed because Plato deems the populace at large as most unwieldy when not managed

19

by a state apparatus that governs the life of the individual so as to keep him from harm to the health of the state. As example, in Plato's estimation the state should raise the children: not the family to whom they are born.

With the exception of some doctrines of the Sophists, like that of Thrasymachus (who sounds somewhat like the later Renaissance political thinker Machiavelli who also equates morality with power), Plato is perhaps the first philosopher of note who takes what could be deemed counterintuitive positions. For example, in his political philosophy, Plato may seem to the modern reader positively at variance with the modern conception and argument for political rule by the people and for the people. On closer inspection of some of Plato's argument, however, we might encounter salient points he makes against democratic rule. We are not required, however, to adopt wholesale or partially for that matter, what he says, simply because he is a great philosopher. In philosophy, in noticeable contrast to most other subjects of study, what may be deemed initially outlandish and bizarre argument can be the order of the day. That is, in philosophy any argument or point or view is allowed its say, but all points of view will be weighed under the purview of reason. This simply means that any point of view that marshals reasons and arguments as support is and should be welcomed in philosophy. Philosophical opinion, however, is not an invitation to a free-for-all (as a beginning student in philosophy might be inclined to think). Rather, philosophy is better conceived as the construction of a courtroom where we weigh contentions, no matter how unlikely they may seem to us in the beginning.

Plato is regarded by some as the greatest philosopher who ever lived, with his student Aristotle running a very close second, if not himself first. Because of the great influence of each of these thinkers upon subsequent philosophers a general understanding of the thought of Plato and Aristotle gives one some understanding of much subsequent philosophy, both of antiquity and the medieval period. That is, until the modern period of philosophy(beginning in the seventeenth century or thereabouts), a good case can be made that most philosophers are generally distinguished by preferring the thinking of one of these two thinkers. Some, like the Roman Boethius (c. 450– 524 AD), think that the thought of Plato and Aristotle can comport with the thought of the other, but such a view to most philosophers of today is virtually impossible to vindicate without substantially minimizing their evidenced differences.

Because of these differences, and some of them substantial, it would be easy to imagine, but wrongly so, that these two men were probably personally and professionally antagonistic toward each other. Moreover, Aristotle was for twenty years a student of Plato in "Plato's Academy," and maintained the highest respect for his teacher. As one sign of this respect, Aristotle did not formulate in writing his dissent with many of Plato's positions until after Plato's death. At the same time, while Aristotle sat under the tutelage of Plato, this aspiring student philosopher was undoubtedly formulating his own conceptions and positions that in time would show Aristotle's departure from his teacher's ideas. As earlier indicated, as distinguished as these two thinkers are, they are also markedly different thinkers and on many philosophical issues they opt for opposite positions. To give only two examples, Aristotle thinks that citizens should have what amounts to the right of ownership of property: Plato, no. Plato thinks that art and artists can be dangerous in society if left unmonitored or uncensored; Aristotle thinks that much art can provide a needful kind of therapy for people.

Plato's philosophy is perhaps distinguished most by his other worldly focus, ultimately presented in his doctrine of the world of Forms, sometimes called Ideas, sometimes Ideals. A Renaissance painter, Raphael (1483– 1520), painted a memorable picture entitled "School of

Athens" which depicts a plethora of ancient philosophers in a variety of postures, but with Plato and Aristotle at the center of the painting. This positioning of the two men in the center is indication of their great influence. Furthermore, to indicate the orientation of Plato's philosophy, Raphael paints Plato with the index finger of his right hand pointing upward to the immaterial Forms. The Forms are in no spatial place because they are not physical things, but Plato's gesture is enough to convey the orientation and emphasis of Plato's philosophy. By contrast, Raphael paints the right hand of Aristotle pressed downward. This indicates Aristotle's philosophy as arising from a consideration of facets and facts about the material world, rather than the immaterial, as in Plato.

Plato regards the postulation of the World of Forms, as odd as this idea may sound to modern ears, as necessary in order to make the physical and material world intelligible, and indeed to account for its reality. Unlike Aristotle Plato places his Forms or models of things in this world in another world, or as Aristotle writes, Plato "separates" the Forms from particular things. For Plato, Forms are essences and constitute what is deemed essential to what a thing is in perfect form. Because Forms are the models from which all things are derivative, this feature of Forms draws out attention to them. However, because Forms are immaterial according to Plato, but because we are in part material beings as humans, grasping Forms is extraordinarily difficult. Indeed, like the prisoners in a cave, we are apt to believe the shadow of a thing is the real thing until we see the thing that is responsible for the shadow. We see this, however, with the mind's eye, not with our eyeballs. This is why Plato oftentimes refers to things in the world as copies, because they are at best facsimiles of that which is perfect and from which particular things are imperfectly modeled. Such an assertion of the dichotomous nature of reality, that is, between the material and the nonmaterial, is at the center of Plato's philosophy. Plato therefore

22

generally views the material world as a lesser world in any comparison to the immaterial and perfect world of the Forms.

The same evaluation is seen in Plato's anthropology of the human person. With reference to knowledge, and by extension to values, the goal is for the mind to discipline the material body, as the body and its accompanying desires only too readily detract the mind from its proper focus. Furthermore, Plato tends to view the human emotions, derivative from the body, as the weakest part of the human person. Plato therefore is not a fan of art nor artists—though he is deeply reverent toward beauty. This is because Plato sees art as interfacing with the weakest part of the human person—the emotions. People, therefore, are immensely culpable before the powers of the artists and art. Furthermore, art has no necessary relationship to truth, and the skillful artist can dupe someone into thinking that the true is the false and the false is the true. However, the appeal of art derives from the cooperating weaknesses of the human person, found in emotion. The power of art is a power that can overwhelm the normal discerning mind with titillations and extravagances that seduce even the rational person.

Plato thus configures the human person in a manner exalting the spiritual quality or potential of the human person for true wisdom. He makes short shrift of the material body; to Plato, "the body is the prison of the soul." Consequently, there are grave tensions within the human person, who must do battle with a soul pinched by the demands and temptations of the body. Indeed, with the greater part of the human person (the soul) in imminent danger from this situation, life becomes a matter of in effect trying to properly place the frequently overpowering body under the rightful rule of the soul. The problem, however, is that the soul is the prisoner of the body. To turn the human person around in such a predicament is no small task, but it can be done and be done masterfully. Socrates's courage at his trial and his martyr's death are illustrative of a successful life lived with just such mammoth courage. Socrates, therefore, manifested indifference toward physical things, bodily death included, for the simple upholding of greater immaterial things and values. This is why Plato can refer to Socrates as the most beautiful person who ever lived, even when by most accounts Socrates was far from physically attractive and ill proportioned. Real human beauty for Plato is in evidence when one lives a virtuous and therefore salutary life against what most people would count as impossible odds.

Plato was impressed by Heraclitus's notion that all things change and agreed with Heraclitus to a point. At the same time, Plato thought that for knowledge to be truly so, it must be certain knowledge, and therefore such knowledge must be a knowledge of things that do not change. Because the material world is in constant change, knowledge of the material world cannot be the touchstone of certain knowledge. As example, to know what beauty truly is, it is necessary to contemplate beyond and behind beautiful things for they diminish as they are only physical. Real beauty is of a kind which never diminishes. Therefore, Plato ultimately points to real knowledge as knowledge of the concept, which alone is perfect and therefore transcends anything physical. In line with this way of thinking, it is understandable that Plato is a great lover of mathematics. That is, the truths of mathematics are not qualified by time, place, or person. The ultimate world of truth is therefore independent of the changing material world we live in. Training in mathematics can therefore provide a window to understanding how the World of Forms exist.

Plato also indicates why such a world is necessary, for the theory of Forms may strike the observer as pointedly odd and even unnecessary, but elements of Plato's predilection to posit such a World of Forms in part follow from reasoning that can appeal to most everyone. To take one example, if a country failed to produce a single copy of its constitution such that none could be found, one would hardly say as a result of such a "missing" document that that country therefore lacked a constitution. That is, the governing logic in such response is that as handy as it is to have a physical document to refer to, the constitution ultimately consists of the ideas enunciated and agreed upon among a group of people. These ideas are not constituted from or by the paper which contains the physical markings representing the ideas. The idea is more fundamental and in this case, its physical manifestation is dependent upon the antecedent idea which may come to paper, but is not constituted as paper. Thus, the loss of the paper would not mean the genuine loss of the constitution. In something of a similar way we talk about seeing into the soul of a person, with the implication, aware of it or not, that we have seen the inner or real person. That real person, moreover, is only partly visible from the outside, though the exterior may be a reflection of the interiority of the person, as when the English poet Edmund Spenser (1553– 1599) wrote that "Of the soul the body form doth take."

1. D. Aristotle

As had Plato, Aristotle (384– 322 BC) comes from a well-to-do family. His father had been court physician to the political ruler Phillip of Macedonia. His physician father is thought to have prompted Aristotle to incline toward the study of nature and of course Aristotle's interest in the material world would be a distinguishing mark between Plato and his most famous student. Even if Aristotle had not established a reputation as one of the greatest thinkers of all time, he would nevertheless merit at least a mention in the annals of history for having been the tutor of the young Alexander the Great, son of Phillip, for three years. So far as we know, however, Alexander bears no noticeable influences from his teacher in his later adult life. We do know, moreover, that Aristotle took issue with Alexander's practice of having some of his military commanders marry princesses of conquered peoples. This may reflect the fact that Alexander had more worldly savvy than his teacher, who thought such practice a marriage of gross unequals and thus a dilution of Greek superiority. With this judgement as example, Aristotle's Greek provincialism is often remarked upon by commentators.

However impractical such disagreement with Alexander may make Aristotle appear on this matter, on matters of philosophy, Aristotle showed something of a remarkable convergence with what we might call common sense or perhaps moderation at various points in his philosophy. We might say Aristotle does not set the philosopher apart from the world, but in the world. As indication, however odd philosophy may seem to many, Aristotle thinks that humans by nature are curious. In other words, though philosophy may find few willing to take it up as the historical philosophers of note have, philosophy—or more the curiosity from which it springs—is not ultimately alien to humans but undeniably natural. Furthermore, showing his views as akin to some common sense, he thinks that the most successful way to inculcate a desirable trait of human character is through practice until it becomes somewhat habitual. Though not identical to it, this idea is not totally foreign to our notion of "Practice makes perfect." He is also famous for his doctrine of the "Golden Mean." With this Aristotle argues that a desirable trait such as courage is what it is because courage is found between two extremes, foolhardy callousness or recklessness and on the other extreme, cowardice. Moderation in Aristotle is generally commendable.

When we make further inquiry into Aristotle's notion of knowledge, however, we see the more technical philosopher and the scientist in him emerge. That is, for him the most desirable knowledge is that which gives us knowledge of why something is what it is, as opposed to a simple acquaintance with the fact that it is. Consideration of this question necessarily draws

Aristotle into his famous enunciation of the four causes as the methodology whereby we give answer to this question. Aristotle wants to know both how and why something is what it is.

On another level, for Aristotle the most desired kind of knowledge is that which we can justifiably use to make cogent generalization possible. This is why Aristotle, like Plato, thinks that the only knowledge actually worthy of the name is knowledge of what they refer to as "universals." Plato dedicates a tremendous amount of energy attempting to enunciate how these universals exist in his theory of Forms. Typical of the empirical side of Aristotle, however, he desists from Plato's idea that they exist in another nonphysical reality, and affirms that the universals exist in the particulars themselves. For Aristotle Forms do exist, just not in the manner in which Plato construed their existence.

Though Aristotle is drawn to consider study of the natural world in a way that Plato is not, at the same time he posits a "first philosophy" (really metaphysics), which attempts to identify the nature of the ultimate features of reality. As a work in metaphysics such philosophy ascends to the highest level of abstraction in order to account for what philosophers of this era and medieval philosophy called "being." With Aristotle's emphasis on analyzing actual and conceptual change in nature compared to Plato's emphasis on the realm of the transcendental, Plato has been characterized as a philosopher of being. Aristotle understandably is often seen as a philosopher of becoming.

Within this context of Aristotle's philosophy, attention must be drawn to his infamous but influential methodology of explanation known as the four causes. Only with the advent of modernity will the influence of Aristotle's description began to wane. The easiest example in which to delineate these four causes, and therefore often used, is that of a piece of sculptured marble artwork. The final sculpted object is the product of (1) the chunk of raw and rough marble

27

the sculptor begins with, called the *material cause*, (2) the template or blueprint in the sculptor's mind of what form he wants the sculpted object to take, called the *formal cause*, (3) hands of the sculptor and his tools for working the marble into shape, called the *efficient cause*, and (4) the purpose for which the object is made, called the *final cause*. Given the object and maker described, Aristotle's explanations seems well fitted.

However, in describing objects in the natural world, explanation of this sort will encounter more difficulty, something which Aristotle concedes in terms of the thing in nature explained. Nevertheless, and especially in terms of final cause, Aristotle maintains that the purposive final cause is evident in the world of nature simply because each thing exists for a specific purpose; a pumpkin plant, for example, has as its purpose that of producing pumpkins. In his contention that things have such purposes Aristotle is what we call a teleological thinker — that is, purpose runs through the being of all things that are.

Furthermore, Aristotle is not hesitant like many of today would be, to further affirm, for instance, that humans too have a purpose or final cause. Aristotle does this quite logically after he has noted that lumber or stone is utilized for the purpose of constructing buildings and like structures, just as the skills of a carpenter, for example, are utilized in building a house or a cabinet. In turning to consider the purpose of a human, moreover, Aristotle looks for what most distinguishes or differentiates the human. The function of the human person is to think, and to the degree that one does this, the human is fulfilling their function. Aristotle defines the human as the "rational animal," and though the use of reason might be shared with other creatures, humans possess the capabilities of reason in the highest degree. Some critics of Aristotle have seen this definition of the function of humans as prejudiced toward the vocation of the philosopher, who of course pursues reason and rationality with fervor.

Aristotle's anthropology is significantly different from that of Plato; Plato's position might be called an adversarial dualism. In Plato's conception soul and body are locked in conflict ultimately not overcome until physical death of the body and readmittance to or rejection and rebirth from the World of Forms. (Plato is one of the very few Western thinkers until modernity who embrace the notion of reincarnation.) Aristotle concedes that the human has conflicts within their person, but his overall description of the human person presents the human in much more unified perspective than Plato. While Aristotle concedes that the soul and body are present with a human, neither has standing or reality alone. While the soul informs or gives order to the body, the soul nevertheless does not usurp the authority of the company it keeps— the body. Indeed, in Aristotle's account the soul does not subsist alone in the absence of the body at death. This is why in Aristotle there is nothing like an extended or even anxious discussion of human immortality. This is in notable contrast to Socrates's discussing whether he will live after death with his friends immediately prior to the deadly drinking of hemlock.

Aristotle, however, does intimate that there is what he calls an "Active Intellect" which is a *nous* or mind that always possesses and exercises thinking. This Active Intellect therefore has no residual potential for thinking, because all is at work and being expended so to speak. Aristotle implies that such a thing, the Active Intellect, is or at least is very like his "Unmoved Mover." This entity could be therefore properly characterized as Deity of a sort. This is also the reason Aristotle describes such an entity as "Thought thinking itself."

Furthermore, Aristotle contends that we are most like this entity when we are engaged in thinking—something that the Active Intellect never desists from, as compared to finite and perishable persons. However, at this point Aristotle does provide a link of sorts between this Being and our being. That is, to the degree that our thoughts rise to its Thoughts, we participate in an immortality of a sort on occasion. Any such participation or nexus of meeting between minds, however, ceases on our demise at death. This is because our Agent Intellect, couched in our soul and making possible the intellectual heights we do attain in thinking, has risen to heights unsustainable when we cease to think because our body has lost in death the form which previously informed our thinking. It would seem to be the case in Aristotle, then, that perhaps a form of pantheism ties us to immortality, in some not very clear manner.

In Aristotle's science he blends to significant degree, science with ethics. This he does by identifying the function of entities in nature and then ascribing to them the property of goodness to the degree that they fulfill this function. So, therefore, a pumpkin plant is good that produces pumpkins. Aristotle's science is therefore again referred to as "teleological" because he ascribes purposes to nature. In modern science, however, allusion to purpose largely evaporates and so too Aristotle's concept of purpose. What happens in nature simply happens. To Aristotle this notion would make little sense.

Unlike Plato, Aristotle has as much place in the history of science as he does in the history of philosophy. This is because Aristotle has a keen eye on the material physical world that Plato does not. Indeed, until modernity, science was Aristotle, at which time, Aristotle's science was for the most part abandoned. Unlike Plato, Aristotle believes the senses provide our access to knowledge. He says "there is nothing in the mind that is not first in the senses." Plato had distrusted the senses because they can be deceptive, as when a pencil appears broken when placed in a glass of water. But for Aristotle, the senses are the key to knowledge of the world. The observation that things change in the material world does not put Aristotle off like it does

Plato. Instead Aristotle devotes a considerable amount of philosophical energy to analyzing cause and change in the material world. In significant ways Aristotle is a philosopher of the world and is interested in virtually everything within it. Aristotle was the first thinker to write about and largely devise formal logic, which, unlike Aristotle's science, is still for the most part around today. With strong justification, he has been called a polymath.

Ancient philosophy after Aristotle changes because the political condition of the Greek city-states deteriorated, and particularly so after the collapse of the Greek empire set in motion by Alexander the Great. With this collapse, philosophy generally retreats to focus upon the individual as an individual. This individual will have to find his way in a much larger world than the picturesque but small Greek city-state. Philosophy will now come closer home—that is, to the human—and further from the cosmological orientation of some prior philosophers.

Chapter 2
Hellenistic Philosophy

2. A. Greek Philosophy

When Aristotle's former student Alexander of Macedonia and his army conquered much of the known world at the time, much of Greek life was transformed. This change in great part came about because the previous close confines of the relatively small Greek city-states, such as Athens, were no longer partitioned off from the wider world, but were significantly thrown into it. The previous divisions and boundaries between the Greek city-states were now politically weakened, not to say dismantled, as all now lived under a larger and more cosmopolitan Empire. The individual would now have to find his place within a variegated world which exposed him to new cultures and thoughts far afield from cozier and previously proud, but sometimes now, uneasy city-states.

At the same time, Greek culture was not moribund and would spread to some of the ends of the earth now a part of Alexander's Empire. Upon Alexander's early death at about thirty-two years of age, what would have been a colossal empire under one ruler was soon partitioned among four. Alexander's generals, Seleucis and Ptolemy, took large portions, the former taking in vast regions of the present day Middle East, to include Jerusalem and the latter taking in much of Egypt. The much smaller kingdoms of Macedonia (weakly defended by Alexander's family) and Greece (where city-states formed defensive confederations with neighbors) fell to the Romans in mid-second century BC. Previously some of the city-states had been great rivals of one another; now some had to band together.

In referring to Hellenistic philosophy during this time we are referring to roughly half of a millennium, from about the time of Alexander, until about 200 AD. For the pervasive influence of Greek Hellenism as a cultural idea and influence, we need not look far. As example, during these centuries there is common reference to the "Hellenists," both Jewish and Christian, in some books of the Christian New Testament. During this extension of Greek ways and culture into the world, there was also the reverse, whereby influences of the east came west. In this amalgamation of greater cultural variety, philosophies appeared with efforts toward stilling some of the tumults of the time.

During this period, absent are the attempts at wholesale cosmological speculations of the type found in the earlier Pre-Socratics. Largely gone too are the epistemological conundrums of a Parmenides and a Zeno, who had previously alleged the impossibility of change. The "flux" highlighted in Heraclitus's notion of the everlasting change present in the world is now visible in new political partitions and factionalisms hardly present during the heyday of Classical Greece. In the mix of ideas and cultures in ferment and largely because of the changes in the political landscape, we find some new philosophies coming to the forefront. Accordingly, these philosophies reflect something more of a practical, that is to say, ethical concern, prompted by living in such a tumultuous world. The situation will scarcely happen again until centuries later when the Roman Empire began weakening and various and new philosophies attempted to provide cover over cultural strife.

Furthermore, with life focused upon such concerns, it is comparatively easy to see how philosophies of the time, directed more toward how to live, would become more religiously orientated, as we see, for example, in Plotinus. Even with a thinker like Lucretius, who is very critical of religion, that criticism is raised from an ethical philosophy attempting to provide composure and peace to the individual, with religion deemed as offering only its opposites. Moreover, with such practical emphases taking center stage in the philosophies of the time, later Roman philosophy, as the Roman Empire establishes itself where previously the Greeks had ruled, will continue in this brand of philosophy. That is to say, the practical orientation of Roman culture only made pragmatic Roman thinkers more readily accepting of Greek Hellenistic philosophy, rather than the previous speculative heights of Classical Greece. Philosophies of the Hellenistic period had already turned attention toward man and his troubles rather than figuring the building materials of the cosmos. The central problem addressed during this period was thus what made for happiness and for ultimate happiness.

One Hellenic and then Roman philosophy coming on the heels of Alexander's newly minted empire was Epicureanism. To this day to call someone a follower of this philosophy is to indicate a person given to pleasures, and probably sensual pleasures for the self. However, the formulator of this philosophy, Epicurus (341– 271 BC), had a very different idea. Epicurus did desire to enunciate the goal of human life, which he did define as pleasure. Epicurus, however, did not believe that the more pleasure the better. In fact, having identified pleasure as the wellspring of human life, he believed realization of pleasure required some restraints so that pleasure did not turn to pain or disappointment. Furthermore, not all pleasures were equal because the ultimate pleasure for Epicurus is a kind of peace and tranquility that would not accompany the satisfying of unrestrained sensual and material appetites.

There is a real sense in which Epicureanism inculcates a kind of stoicism that we find highlighted in the ancient philosophy known as Stoicism, and founded by Zeno (334– 262 BC). The chief difference between these two philosophies, however, is that the tranquility that Epicurus encourages can only come about, according to Epicurus, by humans overcoming the fear of death and fear of God. The tranquility of the Stoics, however, comes about to great degree because of the alignment of the individual with reason and with God conceived as reason. Epicurus was willing to admit that God might be present in reality, but if so God was material like everything else (because Epicurus was a materialist) and more importantly, God was an effect and not a cause. Furthermore, for Epicurus the fear of God detracted from the desired happiness and contentment of the human person. Finally, in Epicurus' materialism, one could and should cease to fear death, with the realization that at death everything ceases to be. There is no pain nor pleasure in this state and therefore nothing to fear because there is nothing after death.

The Stoics were great advocates and admirers of Socrates and forever respected the fortitude and courage with which Socrates faced his accusers and his execution. Socrates had refused to compromise his principles, even to the point of refusing an attempt to escape, because of the implication of guilt such attempt would imply. Furthermore, Socrates was unmoved at the brink of his death, unlike his friends and admirers who wept bitterly when he turned up the hemlock to drink. Stoicism had a brilliant early career and boasts of such luminaries in the ancient world as Cicero and Seneca, the latter as advisor to the infamous Nero the Great (37– 68 AD). The Roman Emperor Marcus Aurelius (121– 180 AD) counted himself among the Stoic number. In the New Testament the Apostle Paul is recorded as speaking before Epicurean and Stoic philosophers (Acts 17:18– 34).

The Stoics admiration for and practice of fortitude in the face of adversity is responsible for our reference to someone as stoical who is unmoved and unflinching in adversity. Not contemptuous of religion or God as the Epicureans tended to be, the Stoics did nevertheless tend to be materialists. Their materialism, however, interfaced with their belief that reason permeated matter, making it intelligible, and that reason was God. God therefore was in all things. The intelligibility of things then was due to the fact that law not chance governed things and matter, and from these Stoics we derive the notion of natural law.

This fixity of nature, in conjunction with the materialism in Stoicism led to a rather deterministic philosophy in which human freedom is problematic. Nevertheless the great Stoic teachers were insistent that the human will can peaceably accept the inevitability of the cosmic law that permeates the world and reality. Human happiness is achieved in accepting rather than fighting against the inevitable.

During this time a group of philosophers referred to as the Skeptics tended to be skeptical toward the philosophy of both the Epicureans and the Stoics, as well as Plato and Aristotle. Their founder was an individual named Pyrrho (361– 270 BC), and the early form of this philosophy was known as Pyrrhonism. Skepticism as a school of ancient philosophy extended into the future for some time, and found perhaps its most worthy exponent in an individual named Sextus Empiricus (about 200 AD), from whom we derive much of our knowledge of this ancient philosophy today.

The ancient Skeptics tended to be just that, that is, skeptical with regard to many contentions of others, and therefore they not unnaturally drew many responses from opponents. St. Augustine wrote against the Skeptics, and Descartes, the so-called father of modern philosophy rose up to defend the claim of knowledge against a revival of ancient skepticism in his modern day. While philosophical skepticism has rights to its claim to be one among a number of philosophical schools, its prominence is most heightened by strenuous antagonism to it from opponents. Opposing philosophers, though usually claiming a contradiction within the skeptical doctrine, more feared the possibility that acceptance of skepticism would entail the ultimate demise of philosophy, or the search for an objective truth. To critics this idea or doctrine was as unnerving as the uneasy world around them. For skeptics, however, the idea meant something else, for Skeptical philosophy was intent to insure mental calmness with the realization that we do not have the last word on anything. The Skeptics therefore tended to be the enemies of dogmatists who claimed certainty on matters which to the Skeptics were a matter of dispute. The Skeptics were not merely skeptics deriving from an unrealistic standard for what would count as certainty, but rather they noticed, somewhat like the Sophists, the tremendous variation among people of how they interpret experience and appearances. Furthermore, because the Skeptics argued that our knowledge derives from our senses and because we know our senses to be deceptive on occasion, we should be cautious about what they confer to us.

With regard to morality, because the Skeptics denied the possibility of knowing there was a natural law pervading reality, as did the Stoics, they tended to hold that there was no absolute moral knowledge. If Skepticism was a philosophy designed to insure mental calmness, it might seem then that as a moral philosophy it would fail. However, the Skeptics asserted that probability was a sufficient guide in moral decisions, and that at the same time, no dogmatism should attach itself to our moral beliefs. Thus, like most of the philosophies of the time, however different in teaching, this philosophy too could ease the difficulties of living in a tumultuous world.

2. B. Roman Philosophy

After the earlier and more stable Roman Republic descended into increasing tumult and leaders with unrestrained ambitions, people living within the Roman domain began searching for solace outside the structures and men of the state. (Rome as a republic is usually deemed to have ended in the first century BC, being followed by the Empire called Roman with the ascent of Caesar Augustus to the throne.) In this climate, the practical philosophies of the day found competition not only among themselves, but encountered and jostled with the so-called mystery religions of the day. Such religions seemed to many to present doctrines and teachings that seemed more satisfying than what the philosophers offered. The emerging Christian religion, beginning in the first century under a Roman Empire rather than a Roman Republic, was one of many mystery religions that in time would supersede others. This religion would thus necessarily draw the attention of the philosophers, particularly as its presence in terms of followers seemed to grow at times exponentially.

When we come to philosophy as it existed in the Empire, we notice almost immediately its political associations. That is, among the Roman philosophers of note, most are aligned with, and sometimes in the employment of the Roman state. This fact is most notable perhaps in the case of Seneca, who was political advisor to Nero the Great (37– 68 AD), the latter of fame for the execution of not a few Christians, to include in all probability, Peter and Paul in about the year 65 AD. Of special note among the many Roman Emperors is Marcus Aurelias (121– 180), a Stoic philosopher and Roman Emperor from 161 to 180, and a critic of the Christians living within the Roman domain. The Roman philosopher of most eminence among his countrymen and of continuing influence after his death, however, was Plotinus, who served as something of a spiritual director to some political men of high station in Rome.

The association of Western philosophers with politics and politicians is not a completely new enterprise starting with the Roman philosophers, such as we find with Seneca. Indeed, one might observe that not a few notable philosophers of history have desired to be influential among the politicians of their day. With and without invitation some took steps in that direction. With such intent, certain risks are evident to the philosopher. That is, in most cases the philosopher could feel the pressure to submit before the greater power of the politician served. Should disagreements arise, the philosopher might be tempted to compromise his integrity out of fear, for conflict might very well send him to his death, particularly in the ancient world. Neither situation appears very welcoming or promising for the philosopher in association with the politician.

However, after the death of Socrates, and probably to escape the stench of political culture in Athens at the time, Plato had sojourned to Egypt and then Italy (where he encountered and was impressed with the Pythagoreans). In the specifics of Plato's case, moreover, and on invitation to come to Sicily as a trusted political advisor, Plato found himself enmeshed in political intrigue and ended up having to take flight. Before matters had become that acute, however, Plato had sensed he was being used for political gain. Plato records something of his resultant suspicions in his Seventh Letter: "Therefore, he [Plato's political patron] made a great pretense of entreating me. And we know that the entreaties of sovereigns are mixed with compulsion." Plato's flight, then, was staged from some distrust of the motives of politicians. Any alliance would have to be for another day. Thus, at about forty years of age, he returned to Athens to start what became famously known as Plato's Academy. Apparently it was the case that running this school was less of a strain than trying to offer advice to a ruler in how to run his country.

Perhaps the most notable historical instance of a philosopher vying for influence upon the apparatus of a state comes from the life of the great Chinese thinker, Confucius (551-479 BC). Wearied over the constant warfare between political factions in the ancient China of his day, Confucius made some extraordinary efforts to ingratiate himself to political rulers but found only intermittent success. With such failures at his back, Confucius seems to have sought solace in his students, who apparently gave more sincere ear to his teaching than political figures. So too like Plato's experience, only more, Confucius had seen his life in danger on not a few occasions from hostile political rulers who perceived in Confucius's thinking a threat to their model of political governance.

When we come to consider the philosophy of the Roman philosopher Seneca (c. 2-65 AD), moreover, we might have opportunity to witness the truths and subtleties of philosophy yielding before the raw realities of politics, given the rather blighted reputation of Nero gleaned from Christian and other sources about this infamous emperor. That is, in this case perhaps we catch a glimpse of how well philosophy and the philosopher fare in the hard world of politics. Indeed, not a few modern critics of Seneca have charged that the man Seneca finessed his Stoic philosophy with too much concession to the hard political demands of Nero's court.

Much in line with previous Stoics, Seneca does not lay out a theory of virtue, but inside provided a program or regimen of practice in virtue. Therefore, we find in Seneca warning of the finite nature of many material goods that cannot elicit the Stoic calm desired. Fame and recognition are but ephemeral glories capable of plunging one into subservience before them, rather than the reverse. Seneca's attachment to a court such as that of Nero has evoked the criticism that the man surely taught one way but lived another. However, one might make the more gracious point that Seneca had overwhelming occasion to witness lives lived for all the wrong reasons, and at the same time, Seneca had to endure that conflict within himself. This is not to say that Seneca was morally pure; it is to say that he knew the strenuousness of such moral struggle firsthand and at a higher level than most.

Seneca tempered the determinism detectable in earlier Stoics by his contention that the human will is capable of willing and living a virtuous life. He is not, however, as some of the Stoics were, prone to an argument leading to a kind of self-aggrandizing self-sufficiency which easily results in contempt for others who are deemed weaker. So too, cognizant of the power of temptations to fell even the man who wills otherwise, Seneca shows sympathy for those who plainly see that their approximation to the desired life of virtue rarely approximates anything near perfection. Certainly not a defeatist, he is nonetheless a realist. On the other hand, solitude of the mystical sort he sees as of little benefit to the making of virtue. (In this he is much like Confucius.) That is, one carries the same self into seclusion that one carries into the company of others. Self-examination is nevertheless encouraged. Such regimen forces the individual to see himself in a way nearly impossible when he lives with diversions distracting from himself.

Marcus Aurelius shared in Seneca's injunction to show mercy for humans wrestling with their weaknesses. Thus, the Stoic is not aloof as pretending to be raising up perfect men, but encouraging aspiring better men to be better. Typical of the Stoics, human floundering and moral missteps are deemed a product of ignorance. Much like Socrates and Plato, as well as Aristotle, this Greco-Roman commitment to inculcating human virtue will clash with elements of later Christian anthropology, but at other times be brought alongside it. Proof that there is a universal commitment to all humanity in some Stoics is that slavery, as a very ancient human practice, was first opposed in the Western world by bands of Stoics. Furthermore, the noted Emperor's work, the *Meditations*, is largely indebted to the ideas of the Stoic freed slave, Epictetus (c. 55– 135 AD). The *Meditations* does evidence some straying from Stoicism in the direction of Platonism, a philosophy that becomes stronger among thinkers as the Roman Empire weakens.

Plotinus stands as a major transition figure between classical philosophy and what was to come in medieval philosophy. His philosophy has an extraordinarily strong religious component, and despite the fact that he lived in the third century (c. 204– 270 AD), at a time when Christian philosophers such as Tertullian (c. 160– 230 AD) and Origen (185– 254 AD) worked, and Christian numbers had become numerous, Plotinus never mentions Christianity. This omission can hardly be indication of anything less than opprobrium for this "new religion" or "mystery religion" and serves as needed reminder that gravitation toward the Christian religion did not occur in a day and neither did it lack opponents for some time after its inception. Of particular note in the case of Plotinus is the fact that his thoughts and writing were of huge influence upon later Christian thinkers, especially St. Augustine, who famously remarks that by change of a word or two in Plotinus's writings, one could see in him a Christian. It is probably safe to say that Plotinus's aversion toward Christianity is fixed around the typical neoplatonic objection to the Christian idea of God becoming man, or the Incarnation.

Plotinus was from Egypt and lived in Alexandria at a time when that city was the intellectual hub of the ancient world. Alexandria also possessed, so far as we know, the largest library in the world at the time, perhaps numbering something like a quarter million volumes. Plotinus studied classical philosophy in Alexandria and gravitated to Plato's philosophy as the surest guide among all the competition. Plotinus, like Plato, took the immaterial soul as primary in terms of what the human person was, and criticized those philosophies, like that of Aristotle, in which soul and body are tied so tightly as to undermine the independence of the soul from the body.

When Plotinus was forty years he went to Rome and opened a school of philosophy. The political bonds of the Roman Empire had of course been weakening for some time, and the religious and moral climate within was extremely variegated. Plotinus, however, attracted attention, and served as counselor of a sort to many prestigious persons in Rome. He also attracted a disciple, named Porphyry (c. 234– 305 AD), who wrote Plotinus's biography, and who also prodded Plotinus into writing down his teaching into the famous *Enneads*. Plotinus numbered among his notable pupils at Rome the Emperor Gallienus and his wife Salonina. Meanwhile Porphyry became busy on his book of objections to the Christian religion, probably under the influence or at least the encouragement of Plotinus in that regard.

Like Plato, Plotinus thought that because the material world was under constant change, it could not be the primary reality. Reality must be unchanging and this is God. Because any creation of the material world would implicate change in God, Plotinus contends that God did not create the world in any ordinary or direct sense. Rather, the world emanates from God, but at some distance. There is a progression of emanations from God, with the first being mind or *Nous*. Mind is therefore immaterial and this is the vehicle for any relationship between the human and divine. Further emanations descend into materiality and therefore are furthest from God. Matter and by implication the human body fall into this category and must therefore be subjugated to a higher end that matter resists.

The human body is therefore in need of disciplined ordering, for the human temptation to evil is a result of a miscalculation that material needs can satisfy ultimate human yearnings. The assent to God is arduous and at times painful because it requires a sloughing off of weighty habits and tendencies keeping us from rising toward the level of mind. The ultimate goal in this journey according to Plotinus is the loss of all particularity. This means the union of the individual, now no longer an individual, is united in union with the One or God. Though the thought of Plotinus would have considerable influence upon the coming age of medieval philosophy, Christian thinkers would nevertheless often exhibit wariness toward this pantheistic implication of the union of the human with the divine.

2. C. *Jewish and Christian Patristic Philosophy*

It is little surprise that Jewish culture produced probing thinkers, for the Jews tended to be among the most literate and most learned among ancient peoples. Furthermore, on occasion the Jews had been exiled, as for example by the Assyrians and Babylonians, and this experience of course gave them wider exposure to the world. Situated geographically as they were— practically in the center of where many empires crossed—they not infrequently had conquerors at their doorstep. Despite, however, these occasions of interactions with other peoples, the Jews for the most part remained astonishingly insular. This demeanor on their part not infrequently drew down the wrath of others who read such a posture as indicative of arrogance or elitism. However, the Jews were recognized for their skills; it is estimated that perhaps ten percent of the work of the administration of the Roman Empire was at various times feted out to Jewish individuals. This, however, probably provoked envy or conspiratorial theories on the part of some attentive Romans.

Indeed, before the Roman presence the Jews, living within the Seleucid Empire, had endured hostilities under the aegis of the Greek Hellenists. At one point Antiochus Epiphanes, a Greek king of the Seleucid Empire for almost a decade, infuriated the conquered Jews with his insistence that Jewish rituals and traditions be abandoned and that the Jews worship Zeus as their primary god. This kind of edict infuriated the Jews and the result was the infamous Maccabean Revolt occurring from 167 to 160 BC. Interesting to consider is the possibility that this overbearing Greek king garnered some of his support from a split within the Jewish community over the incorporation of features of Hellenistic cultural into the insular Jewish religion. Hellenism, therefore, was possibly making inroads to Jewish religious culture, though the community remained divided over the acceptance or rejection of this influence.

Philo of Alexandria (c. 20 BC– 40 AD) is the most notable Jewish thinker of the Hellenistic age. He lived in the same century as the more well-known Jewish historian Flavius Josephus (c. 37– 100 AD), himself a Hellenized Jew, who records many of the conflicts between his community and the Romans. In the days of these men, the Romans were politically in charge of the Jewish world, while at the same time the appeal of Greek ideas, that is to say Hellenistic ideas, was readily accepted for the most part by the Roman world. At issue for Philo, therefore, was how to interface his Jewish religious beliefs, largely deriving from the Jewish Torah of the Old Testament, with his penchant for the Greek philosophy of Plato. Philo makes a valiant attempt. On the one hand he contended (frankly with meager to no proof) that the Greek Pythagoras had been a follower of the Jewish author of the Torah, Moses, and that Plato had been schooled in the school of Pythagoras after the death of Socrates. (Thus, something of a familial relationship was asserted among these traditions.) In such a scenario, then, there was no attempt to force incompatibles to look compatible, but rather the contention that the philosophy of Plato was derivative from the philosophy of Moses. Immersion in the school of one was immersion in the school of the other, for the religion and the philosophy under scrutiny revealed not only a genetic kinship, because one could also by means of allegory interpret many passages of the Torah that appeared at least on the surface, as hardly edifying or the source of any spiritual truth. Nevertheless, for all of Philo's admiration of the Greek philosophers, and particularly Plato, he is unwilling to succumb before a temptation that might overwhelm others committed to Platonism. That is, an individual can be so enamored of a deeper or spiritual meaning of the religious text that any allegiance to bodily or other rituals and ceremonies arguably can be ignored or spurned. This move Philo was unwilling to make; God created man a body and a soul and there are religious acts for both. The human therefore should exercise both in his worship of God. The observed precaution in Philo is commonly lost, however, on other religious thinkers.

In a not dissimilar manner, the early Christian community inherited the debate that the Jewish community had with the Hellenists. That is, Christian disagreement over the compatibility of philosophy and Christian thinking was part of an early debate, extending back to the initial decades of the Christian Church. Like the Jewish community, and sitting on the cusp of ancient Greek and then Roman civilization, the earliest thinkers of the Christian faith had placed themselves at various positions over rejection or assimilation of these intellectually impressive traditions. Augustine, as we shall see, contended that some of the preceding traditions had provided historical stepping stones for and to the Christian message. Others, however, like Boethius, would attempt to bundle up and assimilate prior traditions of the Greeks for Christian use.

Still others like the North African thinker Tertullian (c. 160-c. 235 AD) had retorted to the question with his own question made famous by his wording: "What does Athens have to do with Jerusalem?" So as to make the point of contrast even stronger, he interjected, "I believe because it is absurd." Tertullian is of course casting doubt on the legitimacy of blending two things that he thinks are not capable of mixing, because one will suffer at the hands of the other possibly to the point of demise. Today it is easy to caricature Tertullian's position as seeming to advocate that intelligence and religion cannot be mutual friends, but this would be to misunderstand Tertullian's separation. Tertullian seems to think that reason

47

and philosophy are simply incompetent with things religious, but that in their incompetence they are capable of wrecking what they do not understand, namely religious beliefs. As such, reason is rather like the invading barbarian tribes infiltrating the Roman Empire, and who often destroyed artifacts the Romans left behind because the invaders could not understand how they worked. Thus, religion and religious faith are not without a logic, but it is not a logic penetrable by an ordinary logic or mere reason.

However confrontational this issue was cast, the question remained for thinkers of philosophical pedigree who were now Christian thinkers, over how to estimate intellectual legacies of the past in terms of the Christian present (or Christian theology). Aside from select books of the New Testament—of which not a few predate the Roman destruction of the Temple at Jerusalem in 70 AD—some of the earliest pieces of Christian writing are from the second and third centuries and usually only tangentially speak to this issue. These writing are for the most part responses or attempts at rebuttal of critiques of this new religion in the Empire. Obviously requisite to making such a response was the ability or knowledge of cogently making one's case and this would hardly come from the hands of ordinary laymen. Therefore, though Jesus's disciples were laymen and though they preached their sermons to any and all, the first group of Christian intellectuals, referred to as the Church Fathers, did come from learned society and some with impressive philosophical pedigrees. However, and to our point, the Christian religion came with no partnering philosophy in the beginning. Nonetheless, it is rather obvious that a religion carries with it a group of commensurate or corresponding principles, however implicit they may be. However, such association is rarely so evident as to suggest those associations in the beginning. Thus A. N. Whitehead's useful observation that "Christianity is a religion seeking a philosophy, while Buddhism is a philosophy seeking a religion" points to the surmise that Christianity would historically seek and find philosophical partners in time. Moreover, some intellectual converts were not to be denied interest in the aforementioned issue of possible resonances between the philosophies they may have previously adhered to, in comparison to the new religion they now confessed.

When contemplating Plato's philosophy, some Christian thinkers suggested that in Plato's metaphysical and anthropological orientations in particular there was much that resonated with Christian belief. Any assimilation of one to the other, however, was not due to the perceived weakness of a religion that limped without the aid of such a philosophy. Rather, the thought of Plato had prefigured elements of the Christian philosophy, and the former made for a reception of sorts for a greater truth as found in the Christian Gospel. In a theological way of speaking, God had met some where they were standing. In fact, in St. Paul's famous sermon at Athens, he declares to an audience of Epicureans and Stoics that "Yet he is not far from each one of us, for 'In him we live and move and have our being'; as even some of your poets have said, 'For we are indeed his offspring.'" (Acts 17:27–28).

Nevertheless, the portability of the Christian message among Christian thinkers with other philosophies, even at times with Platonism, remained a matter of debate. Though comparatively few would rally around Tertullian's implied answer in his question of what Athens has to do with Jerusalem, the predominant and friendlier answer to that question allowed many Christian thinkers of later centuries to blend citadels of thought consisting of philosophy and theology. This is most obvious in the example of St. Thomas Aquinas's use of the philosophy of Aristotle.

However, the earliest Christian thinkers had something of a different task in their time as compared to St. Thomas. From the second through the fourth century they had the job of wrestling with able pagan critics of the Christian religion. The Roman Emperor Marcus Aurelias, as one of the latter, and a Stoic, drew a response of Christian defense from an individual named Athenagoras in the year 177. Origen (185– 254 AD), an Alexandrian Christian, and in all probability the most learned in addition to being most productive in writing before the Council of Nicaea in 325, wrote a book of criticism against a Greek philosopher named Celsus who had written a book of criticism against the Christian religion. Perhaps most indicative of the abiding conflict between pagan (or non-Christian) philosophy and Christianity, moreover, is seen in the criticism of Porphyry, the student and friend of Plotinus. Criticisms of the Bible that Porphyry invokes will not be forthcoming again until early modernity. The Christian religion, therefore, hardly gained anything like full assent across Roman culture by the beginning of the fourth century. The next step forward in the history of this mystery religion, however, will be when a Roman Emperor named Constantine essentially adopts that religion and, along with some of his successors, attempts to resuscitate an Empire in great social and political decline.

Chapter 3
Medieval Philosophy

3. A. *Early Medieval Greek and Latin Philosophy*

Historians have long debated when medieval philosophy begins and ends. On first

thought it might seem that medieval philosophy begins its long march with the birth of the

Christian Church. However, substantial time is required before the religious influence of this

religion becomes predominant. Medieval philosophy might be said to begin with St.

Augustine (354 AD– 429 AD), though some historians see him as the last Roman thinker,

that is to say, a classical thinker. Others ascribe the onset of medieval philosophy to a later

thinker, Boethius, with he too often thought of as still substantially a classical thinker. Other

historians of medieval philosophy sometimes opt for a time later than either that of Augustine

or Boethius. This is simply because of the turmoil that made original philosophizing and

philosophical system building extremely difficult during much of their time and for some

centuries afterward. As the Roman Empire in the West began to disintegrate, learning not

only suffered, but the resources for learning lived a precarious existence in the wake of the

Germanic or barbarian invasions. Usually the intent to preserve manuscripts in safekeeping

was about all that could be feasibly accomplished. Original work, which usually requires

resources and some modicum of social order, would be for the future. Because of the

spasmodic bleakness of the age, the entirety of the Middle Ages is sometimes referred to as

the Dark Ages, but this as a term is really only appropriate for select periods of the larger

time-span of the Middle Ages. Nevertheless, when St. Augustine died in 430, the invading

tribe of the Vandals had laid siege to his city of Hippo in North Africa, where he resided, and

Augustine wrote perhaps the first philosophy of history with his *The City of God*. This he did to make sense of the political and social calamity of the time. Much philosophy, therefore, followed the times and tenor in which it was written. Indeed, the life of Boethius about a century later reflected some of the same turmoil, except that by his lifetime, the invading Germanic tribes had started to rule parts of the old Empire assaulted decades before. Boethius in fact worked for a king of the Ostrogoths named Theodoric, who in time suspected Boethius of treason, and had him executed. Nevertheless, and somewhat like Augustine's predicament, while Boethius was in prison awaiting execution, he composed a philosophical classic entitled *The Consolation of Philosophy*. This was perhaps the most read book of the Middle Ages among the learned.

Boethius had earlier worked to translate the whole of the works of Plato and Aristotle into Latin, but only partially finished. His work reflected the fact that among most medieval thinkers, now largely Christian thinkers, there is noticeable attempt to assimilation and to providing a synthesis of Classical and Christian thinking. Thus, Tertullian's question over the congruence of Athens and Jerusalem was largely affirmed rather than denied. In this way, therefore, the main project of medieval philosophy would be to assimilate Christian faith to reason (or philosophy). This effort was expended generally because these medievalists believed in the unity of truth and so truth could be blended into a coherent whole. The question of how far any assimilation could succeed without compromise to the other would prove, however, to be a matter of proverbial concern throughout the Middle Ages. Such worry was renewed in the thirteenth century for those concerned for the integrity of religious beliefs, in light of those thinkers now more than ever concerned for the integrity of philosophical beliefs. With the latter, the religious element in medieval philosophy will be placed on notice and beginning with the Latin Averroists as the University of Paris, increasingly philosophy will go its own way. That is, philosophy will become increasingly seen and defended as an autonomous discipline and no longer remain beholden to religious directives or constraints.

However, in the beginning associations of philosophy with the new religion of Christianity, the lines of distinction were not for the most part adversarial. That is, Christian converts from the class of intellectuals tended to see some previous philosophical thought as anticipating Christian religious ideas, particularly in Platonism. This was particularly true in the Greek East where, for example, the Alexandrian Origen (c. 185– 254 AD) might be rightfully judged the first great systematizer of the Christian religion. However, for all of his intellectual erudition, sometimes Origen's Platonic leanings seemed to move his thinking too close to an emanation account of material reality. More attentive to placing distinctly Christian markers on his ideas was the work of the Greek Church Father, Gregory of Nyssa (c. 335 AD– 395 AD), who might also be called the first systematizer of medieval mystical thought. Gregory enunciates themes, such as the darkness of God and the pursuit of God by the straining human soul that were rich resources for later thinkers, some of whom are much better known today than Gregory. These include Pseudo-Dionysius (Fifth to sixth century AD), St. John of the Cross (1542– 1591), and the contemporary of St. Thomas Aquinas, St. Bonaventure (1221– 1274).

Though Tertullian has rightful claim to being the first and the greatest of the Latin Church Fathers before Augustine of Hippo, it is from the thought and prolific writings of Augustine that the subsequent Western Christian Church drew greatest inspiration. Unlike Tertullian, however, Augustine, like most other Latin thinkers after him, began to ebb in ability to read Greek, the language of the New Testament. Nonetheless, Augustine's

philosophy bears out his distinctively religious and theological interests in a way that is

virtually unmatched by any other Christian thinker of the medieval period. For example, he

gives a distinctively religious priority to the order of knowledge with his famous contention—

shared with the later St. Anselm—that "I believe in order to understand." Augustine is not so

much interested in a synthesis of philosophy and theology, but rather in the way and direction

in which philosophy and hard thinking can point the spiritually hungry to a welcoming God.

This perspective is commensurate with Augustine's own spiritual odyssey from the

Manicheans to Platonism to Christianity. Augustine too, especially in his frank *Confessions*,

links his philosophical quest to the existential anxiety of the wandering and wayward human

spirit. In many places in this work, Augustine sounds very similar to a modern person

searching introspectively to find out who he is. Not surprisingly, *The Confessions* has been

called the first work of modern psychology.

Augustine maintains something of the prior Tertullian distinction between faith and

reason or Jerusalem and Athens in his monumental philosophy of history, entitled *The City of

God*. In this work, written in the context of a crumbling Roman Empire, and in part to answer

pagan critics who alleged the Empire was coming to ruin because of Christian citizens not

paying proper reverence to the Emperor nor to the gods of Rome, Augustine drew a line of

distinction between the City of God and the City of Man. While he advocated no retreat from

the world when that world began to totter, he nevertheless did remind Christians that the

collapsing world was not the sum total of their world, which would persist then and for the

future as the imperishable City of God.

Indicative of Augustine's influence throughout the Middle Ages and beyond, there is scarcely any notable thinker after him who would not find significant points of agreement with Augustine's thinking. Even at the time of the Protestant Reformation, when Protestants began to criticize the mixing of philosophy and theology characteristic of much medieval thinking, the works of Augustine served as a huge resource for Protestant thinkers and theologians countering Catholic thinkers. They equally serve Catholic thinkers seeking to counter Protestants.

In his lifetime Augustine encountered his share of notable opponents, not the least of which was Pelagius (c. 360– 418), a British monk. Actually it was Augustine's writing and preaching that precipitated the dispute with Pelagius. With Augustine's emphasis upon the grace of God, Pelagius deemed Augustine to fall short of encouraging people to extend full human effort toward putting their lives in order. In Augustine's eyes, however, Pelagius compromised the message of the Christian Gospel with his view that the laws of God given to humans implied that they were laws that could be kept. In Pelagius's eyes, Augustine deflected earnest human effort at keeping the laws of God by his notion of the sovereign grace of God. Augustine had other opponents and other controversies, but this controversy with Pelagius became famous, in part because of the implications for human freedom in relation to divine sovereignty.

While Augustine tended to fuse Christianity with many elements of Platonic philosophy, Platonism was brought into the further service of Christian philosophy by the work of Pseudo-Dionysius. The adjective Pseudo is the judgment of later and more severe scrutiny that this thinker was not, as was long thought by medieval philosophers, to include St. Thomas, the disciple of St. Paul the Christian apostle, but an undetermined author writing sometime toward the end of the fifth century. Whatever weight the association with St. Paul may have initially given these writings, the ideas of this author had a life and power of their own. Pseudo-Dionysius moved readers closer to the realm of the mystical, but too close to monism and pantheism for some. Nevertheless, his discussion of our knowledge of God, in the context of the attributes of God, tended to accentuate the differences between God and humans, and if pushed far enough suggested that God might be better known by stipulating what he is not rather than by positive attributions. This suggestion is referred to as the "*via negative*" in medieval thought.

The early medieval attempt for the unity of all truth was not without problems; however, by and large the majority tradition of medieval philosophy was intent on a synthesis of knowledge, and not on separation. Jewish thinkers had tried for much of the same. Philo of Alexandria had made an extraordinary effort to assimilate Platonic philosophy to the Jewish Old Testament, by interpreting the stories of the Old Testament symbolically and with much allegorical interpretation. A much later medieval Jewish thinker Maimonides (1135– 1204) saw in the religious story something of a veneer that springs from a deeper well that remains obscure or even hidden to the ordinary religious believer. It is in part because of the perception that philosophy tends to drain or even destroy religion, however, that a minor, but nevertheless significant tradition in the Middle Ages tends to resist the assimilation of the two. This position is still sharply cast in the infamous question of Tertullian and will be continued to be addressed at points throughout the Middle Ages.

3. B. *Philosophy in the Dark Ages*

The term "Dark Ages" to describe the Middle Ages is misunderstood if assumed to designate an intellectual stagnation brought on by a narrow-mindedness hostile toward thinking. At the same time, it is certainly true that significant stretches of time within the rough millennium of the Middle Ages exhibit a paucity of thinkers. Added to this is the glaring lack of much original thinking and almost no systemization of thinking. That there was something of an intellectual famine at times is unmistakable; a visual survey of the book spines of the *Great Books of the Western World* exhibits this very phenomenon. After a volume dedicated to some of Augustine's writings, the set jumps almost eight centuries to include two volumes of the writings of St. Thomas Aquinas. One can certainly complain that additional volumes, dedicated to John Scotus Erigena and Anselm of Canterbury, might have deserved inclusion. Nonetheless, so many centuries with so few significant thinkers requires explanation.

We have already indicated the social and cultural upheavals evident in the lives and in some of the writings of Augustine and Boethius, principally *The City of God* and *The Consolation of Philosophy*. The impetus to write both of these books in both Augustine and Boethius was prompted by living on the cusps of tumultuous times, for during their days, the old *Pax Romana* (peace of Rome) increasingly decreased. Not even the imperial city of Rome was safe from siege and seizure by the advances of barbarian troops threatening to usurp and overrun the now tattered Empire. The psychological strain of this time must have been on occasion as severe as the physical strains of watching society visibly falling apart. Very few persons would have been exempted from such tumult to one degree or another. The normally contemplative and even sedate lives of the philosopher and thinker did not go unaffected.

The monasteries of the time oftentimes provided the only suitable though not always secure environment where learning had any chance of success, albeit small. The susceptibilities of even monastic communities, moreover, proved just how vulnerable were all things. These monastic communities or "islands of civilization" could fall before a train of invaders such as Islamic armies of the eighth century or the Norsemen in the ninth and tenth centuries. With no armaments with which to protect themselves from such marauders, the monks saw their wealth pillaged and their lives imperiled—and very often taken— trampled under the advance of these Scandinavian warriors.

The Vikings, moreover, in the ninth and tenth centuries were but only the latest group of foreign invaders to imperil much of what at one time, though many centuries before, was the relatively secure Roman Empire. Moreover, as far back as the first century, the Roman establishment had started to crack and by the century after Constantine, the fifth century, the vestige of what had once been the pinnacle of Western civilization to date was in virtual free fall. A half century after the death of Augustine, a barbarian army besieged the previously glorious city of Rome, and the barbarian general in command demanded that he have the honor of the position of Emperor rather than the Roman designee. The barbarian won and the Roman candidate lost.

For people of the Empire, such a transition, coupled with the shows of force exerted by these barbarian bands, represented nothing less than cataclysm. It is scarcely any wonder, then, that in the time of Augustine, many resistant pagan Romans faulted declining worship of the old Roman gods for such disasters. The further charge of some was that the worship of the new Christian God was the source of such downward spiral of their once proud Empire. Little wonder that Augustine felt compelled to respond to this pagan version of the meaning of events in the Empire. Nevertheless, when the fabric of the Empire increasingly fell apart, both Christians and non-Christians tended to see in it the virtual end of the world. Not, however, Augustine.

58

In 529 a monastery was built at Monte Casino in Italy by a religious order of monks, called the Benedictines, taking their name from their founder, St. Benedict (c. 480– 547). From this monastery would come countless others. Issuing from these monasteries would come libraries, however small in the beginning. Also within the monastery was usually a scriptorium, which made copies of books borrowed from other monastic libraries. Books in such a time were precious items, though only a few—usually monks and government officials —could read. The centuries from the inception of this first Benedictine monastery and for about a half millennium afterward are sometimes justifiably called the "Benedictine Centuries." Such attribution is due to the fact that this order maintained, carried, and often protected the vestiges of the past for the present. Without such efforts and dedication from these "islands of civilization" protecting the legacy of a glorious past, there would scarcely have been any knowledge of the past.

Meanwhile, in the same year, 529, the Emperor in the East at Constantinople had Plato's Academy in Athens closed. Modern historians have been understandably quick to castigate this action, though oftentimes presuming the motivation of religious bigotry for the action. That is, closure of the Academy might have been an implicit admission that Eastern Christian thinkers simply could not compete with the largely areligious academics at the Academy. Therefore, to forestall a victory by the competition, one simply does not allow him to compete. It is true that the defrocked teachers went to Persia for employment afterward. However, it is surely possible that with Plato's Academy the Emperor had other motivations, more complicated than any simple narrow-mindedness. One substantial and complicating factor was the fact that "paganism" lived longer in the Eastern Roman Empire than in the West. This is somewhat paradoxical because the Emperor Constantine had built the "New

Rome" in Constantinople in the East, precisely because pagan resistance to the idea in Rome and the West was too strong. That is, though Constantine brought Christianity to bear upon the governing men of state and mechanisms of the state, the legacy of Hellenism nevertheless survived and remained in more than closeted pockets of the Eastern Empire. The Emperor Justinian's action was thus probably one of simple but persistent annoyance with this group, rather than fear that no Christian intellectual could hold a candle to the Greek fire. That is, it was not that he needed reprieve from sleepless nights fearing that thinkers at the Academy would dethrone Christian ideas unless he struck first. They and their predecessors had, moreover, been around for many decades and left untouched.

The insertion of Islam into the Western world created yet another cataclysm during the Middle Ages. However, in terms of intellectual advantage, there were sizeable gains in the confrontation with Islam. That is, in the burgeoning expansion of the Islamic Empire, there had occurred capture of areas of the East like Syria, whereby Islam became heir to much of the classical Greek heritage preserved in such places. In sufficient time, such captures would permit Islamic scholars, after translating the original Greek into Arabic for themselves, to possess an unmatched literary inheritance compared to the meager Greek inheritance held by the West. The inheritance in the West had been hugely compromised simply because of the devastations of previous Germanic invasions, and closer at hand, by the fact that by this time most Western scholars could no longer read Greek.

The West's eventual awareness of the Islamic possession of the works of Greek philosophers, moreover, was slow. Some Westerners became aware of the fact through visitation to Islamic Spain. Others interfaced with the Islamic world through the ventures known as the Crusades, largely taking place in the twelfth century. Previously, however, and on the

60

political front, in 732 Charlemagne's grandfather, Charles Martel, would stop further advance of Islamic armies into the West, so as to prevent the already colossal Islamic Empire from growing any larger. The beginnings of the Islamic Empire dated from the lifetime of an Arab named Mohammed, who died in 632. Like Charlemagne in the Christian West, Mohammed too was functionally illiterate.

From the time of the fifth century a true Dark Age persisted in the West for the ensuing three centuries until the reign of the Frankish King Charlemagne (742– 814), grandson of Charles Martel. With an impressive family lineage and dedication to aiding and supporting the Western Christian Church, Charlemagne was crowned Holy Roman Emperor by Pope Leo III on Christmas Day in the year 800. To many this seemed like the resurrection of the earlier but lost Empire and the heightened anticipation of better days to come must have prevailed in some minds. The intervening centuries between the fall of the Empire and Charlemagne had produced scant philosophy, until the work of Johns Scotus Erigena (817– 877), made possible in part because of the calmer social and political climate created by Charlemagne. Boethius was perhaps the medieval philosopher most under the influence of Aristotelian philosophy up until the time of St. Albert the Great, the teacher and mentor of St. Thomas. But when John Scotus Erigena, the chief figure from the Carolingian Renaissance, enters the scene, and as a translator of some of the works of Pseudo-Dionysius, Platonism will again be in the foreground of medieval thinking.

Charlemagne was more than a man wielding a sword. After his military successes provided some stability and greater peace for his Empire, Charlemagne established a school where his designees worked toward establishing a more learned clergy and the improvement of fledgling scholarship. Interestingly, Charlemagne's responsibility for this enterprise would later be termed by historians as the "Carolingian Renaissance," though issuing from a man unlearned himself and practically illiterate. In time his school stood as a place where scholars of particular note were invited, and where the scriptorium of this complex made copies of the classical Greek and Roman documents they possessed. Historians estimate that perhaps as much as ninety percent of what we possess today are due to the labors of these copyists at Charlemagne's school. Knowledge of past history oftentimes hung by a tiny thread during times of tumult.

With another Dark Age setting in after the collapse of Charlemagne's Empire due to the Scandinavian invasions, not until Anselm of Canterbury did thinking exhibit another high point in medieval philosophy. Anselm, like Augustine, was a high churchman, and like Augustine also, he was also a first-rate and original thinker. Though named Archbishop of Canterbury in 1093, his duties did not circumscribe him to only priestly duties; Anselm imbibed and forcefully expanded upon Augustine's famous injunction to believe in order to understand. Anselm, moreover, goes beyond Augustine and others in philosophical daring. He accepts Christian religious doctrine with humble and pious faith, but he also meditates upon it to the point that the character of God and beliefs of religious faith become transparently evident to him. In other words, he does not reason out the faith before having faith, but having faith and applying one's reason to it, makes an enviable and previously hidden understanding possible. Reason seen in this light, therefore, is no foe of faith, but in many ways explicator of the antecedent faith; reason is thus not used by Anselm to unravel faith, but to penetrate to its cores. Indeed, later medieval thinkers will sometimes surmise that perhaps this method penetrates too far. However, though it is a kind of religious rationalism, it is not a rationalism which undermines religious belief, but one that reinforces it.

Perhaps the best example of this method is not to be found in Anselm's famous ontological argument for the existence of God, an argument developed from a prayer, according to Anselm, but rather in his *Cur Deus Homo*, or *Why God Became Man*. In this work Anselm claims that a proper understanding of God and God's purposes would have made possible a prediction of the Incarnation. Why? Because God's purposes for humanity were thwarted by the sin of the first Adam, and God was consequently under necessary compulsion to Himself to accomplish what he had started, botched though it was by the tragedy of the first couple. A second Adam, therefore, is required to restore God's original purpose. The logic of God, therefore, is evident in the action of God, such that what happens *a posteriori* (after the fact) can be reasoned out or to beforehand *a priori* (prior to the fact). Similarly, in the ontological argument, it is the necessary logic of God's mode of existence that portends, indeed proves God's actual and real existence. The cogency of this argument, to this day, is still hotly debated.

3. C. *Islamic Philosophy*

Because of interrupted efforts in times of social turmoil and the consequent patchy intellectual edifices of the earlier Middle Ages, some historians contend that the beginning of medieval philosophy commences rather far beyond the centuries of Augustine and Boethius. That is, only after the assimilation and digesting of the works of Aristotle by the Latin West in the thirteenth century, or perhaps a bit earlier with the work of St. Anselm (1033– 1109), does medieval philosophy come into its own. The rationale for this late date follows from the fact that the resources of ancient or classical philosophy, previously only sketchily available, are now in place for medieval thinkers. Furthermore, there is now a relatively peaceable world making such an intellectual enterprise possible. Indicative of this social and cultural peak, at this time the great cathedrals of Europe start to rise out of the earth that had previously been given to the ravages of war and conflict. In 1163 construction on the Notre Dame edifice in Paris began; construction of the Cologne Cathedral in Germany began in 1248; construction of Burgos Cathedral in Spain began in 1221; construction of Milan Cathedral in Italy began in 1386.

Even before Anselm, some Islamic philosophers were already wrestling with the works of Aristotle that the Latin Christian West had yet to encounter. Indeed, Muslim philosophers like Avicenna (980– 1037) and Averroes (1126– 98) had written commentaries on Aristotle's philosophy and these commentaries came with the works of Aristotle recovered by the Latin Christian West in the 13th century. Like the Christian philosophers, however, these Islamic thinkers had an eye on their religious faith while they did their philosophy. Thus, Islamic philosophers were engaged in something of an uneasy balancing act between the Koranic revelation and the reason of Aristotle. In addition, because these Islamic thinkers had more of the works of Aristotle in their possession than the Christian Latin West, the strain between philosophy and their religion would become evident to them sooner than it would to the West.

The Aristotelian corpus, beyond Boethius' translations of primarily Aristotle's logical works, finally began to trickle into the Latin West through translators in the thirteenth century. Some works of Aristotle found their way out of Greek through translations into Arabic first made by Syrian Christians centuries earlier. However, in part because some Platonist works, such as a compilation of three chapters of Plotinus' *Enneads,* were erroneously attributed to Aristotle, the interpretation of Aristotle by Islamic philosophers often had a neoplatonic bent. The themes of emanation and illumination are therefore often encountered in

64

their writings.

As much as the thought of Aristotle was prized and studied by Islamic philosophers, the difficulty of interpretation proved to be a serious obstacle to incorporating his thought with religious thought. The great Islamic philosopher of the East, Avicenna (980– 1037), famously commented that though he had read the *Metaphysics* of Aristotle forty times, he only came to understand it after reading a commentary on the work by his predecessor Alfarabi, who had died in 950. All that Aristotle thought, moreover, was not so easy to interface with religious Islam. Because Avicenna contended, among other things, that God created the world from eternity and from necessity, and because God was immaterial, God could not create material things directly, Avicenna found himself at variance with the *Koran*. Though he attempted reconciliation, a successor, Algazel (1058– 1111), argued that both Alfarabi and Avicenna were too wide of the mark of Islamic religious orthodoxy. While Algazel viewed the attempt at the fusing of reason and revelation as certainly permissible, he claimed to find in his predecessors epistemological mistakes which forced them to unnecessarily dispute doctrines of the Islamic faith. Partly out of his frustrations with the enterprise as conceived by his predecessors, he turned to mysticism and a life of asceticism and sometimes solitary contemplation. He even went so far as to write a book provocatively entitled *The Incoherence of the Philosophers*. The most famous of the Islamic philosophers, Averroes, however, sided with the philosophers criticized by Algazel, and wrote a response stingingly entitled *The Incoherence of the Incoherence*. The thought of Algazel, moreover, became a substantial resource for Islamic mysticism, called Sufism.

The response and reaction of the Islamic thinker Algazel would not be dissimilar to the earlier and persisting response of some of the spiritual traditions of the Latin Christian West.

The entry of the works of Aristotle in the West added to a methodology already evident in the rising universities of the Middle Ages whereby disputation assumed a highly organized format for debate and an often exhausting debate. This "scholasticism" found ready critics, who saw in it little of the true religious spirit. Furthermore, not infrequently assertions were made that the most astute thinkers of the time were challenging the boundaries of religious orthodoxy in their hard thinking. An equally frequent charge was that the way of the intellectual with religious faith proved to be only an intellectual exercise with no profit to the soul.

As example of this latter accusation and debate, St. Bernard of Clairvaux (1090–1153), a most prominent member of the Cistercian monastic order, threw himself into argument with a proud and schismatic scholastic, Peter Abelard (1079–1142). Bernard insisted that scholastics were wrongly inclined to knowledge for the sake of knowledge, which to Bernard was to say for the sake of vanity. Bernard held up the writings of earlier Christian thinkers—the Church Fathers and not the scholastics—as his spiritual rudder. Bernard desired a Christian piety that made for godly living, not proud thinking.

Of course such a disagreement between the scholastic tradition and the spiritual traditions of the European Middle Ages reflected much of the earlier debate about the interface between classical thought and Christian thought. This debate we recall extended as far back as the initial decades of the Christian era. Sitting on the cusp of ancient Greek and then Roman civilization, the earliest thinkers of the Christian faith had displayed both attitudes of rejection and assimilation of these traditions, though largely the latter. With the fuller reception of the works of Aristotle now in the possession of the West, this debate would only intensify, and much of that debate was winnowed through Islamic thinkers who had seen and studied Aristotle first. Most of the Islamic commentaries on Aristotle, furthermore, had interpreted him in such a way that his thinking seemed even harder to reconcile with religious orthodoxy than initially surmised. This is why, for example, some Christian thinkers, notably St. Thomas Aquinas, while making use of these Islamic commentators on Aristotle, will also not infrequently take issue with their interpretation of the Greek thinker.

The extension of the Islamic empire to the Roman West, beginning in the seventh century, had in time produced an extraordinary culture and civilization in the province of Iberian Spain, and from here perhaps the most prominent medieval Islamic philosopher of all, Averroes, was born at Cordoba in 1126. Averroes was of the view that Aristotle's philosophy was the unmatched pinnacle of human reason and he set himself to writing commentaries on many of Aristotle's works. As mentioned, these commentaries would be hugely influential for interpreting Aristotle when Aristotle's larger corpus finally came to the Latin West, simply because the commentary could serve as introduction to understanding the formidable Aristotle. Again, however, in time the interpretation of Aristotle's thinking found in these commentaries would be disputed by some—like Thomas—while others were insistent that the commentator Averroes was correct on Aristotle. While Aquinas would be the Christian philosopher generally remembered as making the most use of Aristotle for purposes of Christian philosophy, there would be equally strong advocates for Aristotle alone. Known as the integral Aristotelians, and sometimes, as a tribute to Averroes, as Averroists, Aquinas would oppose them at the University of Paris.

Dispute in the Islamic world over Averroes would later portend a similar reaction to the Christian Averroists at the University of Paris in the Condemnation of 1277 issued by the bishop of Paris, at least for a time. However, in the fourteenth century the persistence of courting Aristotle's way of thinking became too large and powerful for containment by such edicts. Before this, however, the reception of Aristotle's ideas had been divisive among scholars, while the factionalism over Aristotle tended to follow to some degree the religious orders established and firmly in place by this time. The Franciscan order had come into being in 1210 and the Dominican order in 1216. In a relatively short time, these orders produced some of the most notable giants of late medieval philosophy, but before their renown as some of the greatest philosophers of this era, there was opposition. That is, the right of men of the religious orders to teach at the University of Paris was feverishly disputed. They were opposed by the main teaching faculties at the University, and it was finally only intervention by the Pope himself that enabled the religious orders to win, but not without future fights that would erupt occasionally.

St. Thomas, the Dominican, was more receptive to using Aristotle than the Franciscan Bonaventure, but the two joined forces to maintain the establishment of academic chairs for their respective orders at the University of Paris.   While Dominicans like St. Albert and St. Thomas were openly receptive to using Aristotle, the Franciscans, led by St. Bonaventure, were much more guarded in their use of him. In part Thomas and the Dominicans had to endure an Augustinian criticism that in effect lumped them with the Averroists because both made use of and had sympathy for Aristotle's writings. This was despite the fact that Thomas in particular opposed the Averroist party at Paris and particularly the leader, Siger of Brabant (c. 1240– 1284). However, because the Dominicans, like the Averroists, had more recourse to Aristotle, it was guilt by association. Furthermore, Thomas himself was not free of criticism within his own Dominican order and it took some time after his death in 1274 before Thomas's thought could without risk be approvingly called Dominican thought.

The contentions of the Latin Averroists to some degree pointed to the end of the long desired union of philosophy and theology conspicuously evident in medieval philosophy. (As will be indicated in the next section of this chapter, the thoughts of William of Ockham provided another way of ending the union.) The Averroists tended to not exhibit the theological hesitations of others over the credibility of the pagan Aristotle, while at the same time probably disingenuously opting for prudent deference to religious and theological requirements when required. They were by and large content to do philosophy and to report and respect the results of reason on philosophical matters. When Christian belief was deemed conflicting with Aristotle, the Averroists tended to retort that they were simply reporting on the issue from the side of philosophy, that is, Aristotle. It was simply a matter of cultural time before theological belief and theological censure would not be strong enough to keep philosophy within the control of theology, as it largely had been during most of the Middle Ages. Indeed, in the coming epic of modernity theology would be under the firm control of philosophy. What was once the "Queen of the Sciences" would end as a handmaiden (and not even that for some) for philosophy. Tertullian's fear over the conflict of Jerusalem and Athens found some plausibility in this episodic event.

3. D. *The Faltering of Medieval Philosophy*

When St. Thomas (1224– 1274) was dubbed the "dumb ox" by fellow students, his teacher, St. Albert the Great (c. 1200– 1280), warned them that one day they would witness the world gasping while the ox bellowed, for Albert recognized the gifts of his precocious student. Albert's prize student did not disappoint. Thomas took up Aristotle's philosophy for the use of Christian philosophy and theology, and since that day the philosophy of St. Thomas Aquinas has scarcely been ignored, though studied at some times more than others. Indeed, in

1879 Pope Leo XIII in his Encyclical *Aeterni Patris* started a modern revival of Thomism. That revival is for the most part spent these days; philosophers who identify themselves as Catholic are not dominated by any majority of Thomists today. To some degree, however, this phenomenon perhaps attests to the vitality of Catholic philosophy.

Like his teacher Albert, Thomas set upon using Aristotle's philosophy as a viable but not uncorrectable resource for formulating Christian philosophy. As indicated previously, the interface of the philosophy of Aristotle with Christian thinking was fraught with much controversy surrounding "The Philosopher," as Thomas honorifically referred to Aristotle. To many Augustinians in principle this kind of interface could not work. This enterprise would require fitting one to the other and this could not be done because they had not been made for each other. While Thomas conceded there was not mutual compatibility on all points, it was also simply the case that Aristotle's philosophy could be used to explicate portions of Christian thought, without harm to it: not on all points, but on many.

St. Bonaventure took issue, however, charging that Aristotle's views were necessarily not only incomplete with reference to Christian theology, but at odds with it on other points. These "other points," such as Aristotle's beliefs in the eternity of the world and a perceived lack of personal immortality at death, would be condemned as Averroist in the 1277 condemnation, and Aquinas would argue against them and against Aristotle on these issues. However, for Aquinas, Aristotle was more useful than not and one of the ways in which Thomas would use Aristotle, for example, was to use Aristotle's distinctions between form and matter, substance and accident to explain what occurs in what would come to be known as the theological doctrine of transubstantiation. Where Thomas followed Aristotle particularly in epistemology, Augustinians objected, for Thomas appeared to "naturalize" epistemology.

That is, he removes the specifically religious elements of epistemology that had been integral to the account of knowledge as Augustine had described the process; there was no reference to divine illumination, as in Augustine and other Augustinian thinkers.

On the other hand, St. Thomas provided a crisp distinction between philosophy and theology, as it concerns the issue of knowledge. He is unapologetically willing to concede that special revelation as found in Scripture provides us with knowledge about God and ourselves that our reason alone cannot. This does not mean that such truths are unreasonable. The knowledge that the Christian Godhead is a Trinity is an example. However, other matters of what God "publishes" in special revelation could be known by reason, but God puts such in Scripture, for example, so that no one through lack of time or intelligence will miss these truths of God as they pertain to us. The rationale is that these truths are about humankind's ultimate end, which is communion with God. As this is no small matter, it is something vitally important for humans to know such things.

However, whereas Thomas tended to look for identity between reason and revelation, later thinkers will highlight contrasts. Duns Scotus (1265– 1308) and William of Ockham (c. 1290–1349), both Franciscans, are in this camp. Ockham is the more severe critic; indeed Ockham is not a quiet critic of his predecessor Scotus. Nevertheless, these two thinkers and their followers make a pronounced distinction between reason and revelation more accentuated than that expressed by the Latin Averroists. However, Scotus and Ockham proceed from another direction. That is, whereas the Latin Averroists had obliquely given deference to philosophy over theology (or reason over revelation), Scotus and Ockham reversed this by insisting upon deference to theology over philosophy (or revelation over reason).

Scotus had begun to impugn the notion that the discovered rationality of the world is somehow necessary. What we now call laws of nature because of the regularity observed is in fact for Scotus contingent upon the Creator and Sustainer God who can revoke and change the world as he wills. God is under no interdict imposed by his own creation. Thus God is free in his actions, and certainly not living under the encumbrance of any necessary reasons by which he is chained. Thus, Scotus exhibits adherence to the voluntarist tradition of philosophy, where the will of God has primacy over the so-called mind or intellect of God. This importance given to the will of God gives emphasis to the freedom or latitude of God, with the result that the nature of reality is radically contingent or conditioned by the will of God. If this is the case, then *a priori* reason is hardly a ladder or map back to God. The only really reliable map we have is the Christian Scriptures.

Furthermore, with Scotus and Ockham the relationship between the human and God is a covenantal and not a metaphysical relationship. This means that the relationship of the human to God is not analogous to that of a child to parent, but analogous to that of a spouse to their partner. This configuration, however, is not intended to make the human equal to God, but to understand the glue that makes the relationship possible. That is, in the covenantal relationship there is no genetic or physical or metaphysical bond, but rather one of words and agreements. The relationship is in a sense more intimate and more personal, but also, and importantly, at one level more precarious.

In line with this kind of reasoning, Ockham strenuously objected to the "necessatarianism" of some medieval philosophy, because it implied that God exists and operates under what amounts to constraints constructed and presumed by humans upon God, such as goodness. By contrast Ockham emphasizes the freedom of God against the rationalist penchant to define God as a Being wrapped in and beholden to reason. To Ockham, if God is so wrapped with reason, it is with his own reason. In this manner, then, the ways of God are simply past finding out, but can be found in Christian revelation, not human reason. That same freedom of God extends to a divine– human relationship where God is completely, we might say, spontaneous—that is, free to do as he wills—in his relationship with humans. There is therefore no mediating "good," for example, that stands between the two, such that God (like us) must answer to some entity higher than himself. It is not unlikely that in this scenario, God may appear to some as "irrational."

At the same time, however, the Ockhamist insistence upon the individual, and the experience that mediated knowledge, would prove as beneficial for scientific study of the world as it might seem detrimental for the theological method of medieval philosophy. Ockham's insistence upon the "freedom of God" would make *a priori* theology difficult, and force a fresh but required look at a world that God had created. The fresh look would tend to boost the empirical mindset. That is, knowledge is acquired as a result of acquaintance with the world, not theorizing in abstention from it. Scrutiny of the world, rather than intellectual contemplation of the world, might provide a better, and certainly closer, that is to say, truer account of the world. Similarly, to know the mind of the Maker would require more reading exercises with Scripture than thinking exercises. This would prod more looking at the Word of God and the world of God. In their separate but similar ways, this mode of thinking would contribute in substantial ways to both the Protestant Reformation and the Scientific Revolution.

Growing up alongside the medieval philosophical traditions had been the common belief that real religious devotion resided in praying and in the heart, rather than in the exercises of the head and thinking. This way of thinking in time found articulate voices in notable medieval figures who found themselves particularly opposed to Scholasticism, such as we earlier saw in St. Bernard. Such conflict was therefore no mere conflict between "town and gown" as the English university cities of Cambridge and Oxford sometimes exhibited. That is, sometimes this debate found both disputants inside the universities. This fact signifies that the debate was not simply a conflict between the traditional animosities of a lay mindset poised in opposition to the headiness of those within the university.

Part of this debate can be seen in some of the medieval thinkers previously discussed. St. Augustine's Platonism, as example, produced a contemplative bent that inclined some Augustinians in the direction of mysticism, such as St. Bonaventure. Bonaventure, however, nevertheless managed to also live with the other reasoning minds in his environment. His dispute with St. Thomas over the proper uses of Aristotle, however, show Bonaventure more concerned with preserving truth rather than advancing Christian thought through the means of Aristotle.

Jean Gerson (1363– 1429) was himself a chancellor of the University of Paris, but a severe critic of the unionization of theology and philosophy which he characterized as more an intellectual exercise than the result of a heart-felt faith. While Gerson was not critical of knowledge per se, he desired more than cerebral speculations and abstractions. Gerson was careful to keep everything together, the head and the heart, the intellect and the affections; other critics moved to a position that loudly derided an intellectual effort that these critics claimed did not move the inner self. While an anti-intellectualism had surfaced sporadically throughout the medieval period, it now began to flower in earnest as the synthesis of knowledge developed at the summit of medieval philosophy began to topple at the hands of

Scotus and Ockham. Events were coming together so as to topple the medieval attempt at a fusion of Christian faith and philosophical reason.

Mystical inclinations and a religion of the heart found greatest audience outside the universities. This "new" thinking sometimes manifested itself in devotional works in the community at large, such as found in the Brethren of Common Life in northern Europe. To the south, there would be the mystical St. Teresa de Avila (1515– 1582), who managed to develop to an extraordinary level both the inner life of the mystic and the outer life of community service.

If the medieval world had been solidified in the oftentimes precarious and contentious union of Church and State, the unraveling of that union would ultimately in future time put states in charge of the Church in their state. Before this reality would start to take practical shape in the West, however, medieval political thought would have to impugn the Augustinian notion that the state existed for the Church, and that the state existed to provide a curb on sin. Referencing Aristotle again, medieval thinkers, and St. Thomas included, would put the origin of the state not in sin but in the sociable nature of the human. This theoretical contention, however, even as it was developed in thinkers like Marsalis of Padua (c. 1275–c. 1342), would be strongest when the sins of the Papacy appeared most in evidence. By the end of the medieval period, then, we begin to witness a contest of wills between popes and national sovereigns, particularly with the English and French kings. Even William of Ockham the Franciscan would enter the fray over the question of the authority of the papacy in secular affairs, to the point that figments of the notion of a secular state are set in motion. The Middle Ages were creating ground for the coming modern age on multiple fronts and certainly not least of all in political philosophy.

Chapter 4
Philosophy in the Renaissance and Reformation

4. A. Philosophy of Southern Europe

Generally when historians of philosophy come to the Southern or Italian Renaissance, they find difficulty in pointing to who or where are the notable philosophers of this time. In great part this difficulty bespeaks the splendor of extraordinary works of Renaissance art, many of them still visible today, such that the philosophical thinking of this magnificent age seems periphery or secondary to this period. That is, the stunning works of art by the likes of Michelangelo and Raphael, breathtaking architecture like that of Bernini and Brunelleschi, and burgeoning science and art such as found in the fingers and sketches of Da Vinci, seem to place paler items in the background. There are, however, thinkers and philosophers of this period whose ideas literally do break some of the boundaries of previous thinking, such as Machiavelli in political philosophy and Petrarch in what might be called a new conception of the human person.

At the time of the Italian Renaissance there is something of a realization that something new is happening in the world. Furthermore, many surely thought that much of what is new should have happened much. Such thoughts would help account for much of the disdain with which men of the Renaissance viewed the prior Middle Ages. The Renaissance is a proud time and hopes and aspirations are optimistic and many gigantic. The surge of things new and different might justify a description of the Southern Renaissance as an exercise of new possibilities brought into a new world weaning itself from the past.

Of course we must exercise care with reference to the word *new*, for the upward spike of the Renaissance in Western culture took much of its direction and impetus from the classical period of Greek culture. This chunk of Greek history Western culture has never ceased to admire. That being said, we might conjecture that the rise of new national powers, such as that found in the powerful Italian city-states, would permit experiments of individual thinking and doing with few precedents in Western history before the Renaissance. The Carolingian Renaissance of the eight century and the twelfth century medieval Renaissance, both duly noted, can hardly hold a candle to this one. That is, in many ways these prior instances of any Renaissance are simply backdated as tepid antecedents, after this Renaissance of early modernity arrives. That is, the previous two were but tiny glimpses after witnessing the current one. To this day, this Southern or Italian Renaissance remains a marvel to all who study its energies and accomplishments. In many ways it seems to free the human spirit; for some, however, it seemed to imperil too much of the past.

Within this majestic juncture of Western history, the philosophical thinkers collectively share in no single and predominating school of thought. Except perhaps in something of a near universal disdain for philosophical method in the medieval millennium behind them, there is considerable variety in the schools of thought of this time. Within the negative consensus about the generalized past, however, there is a most notable exception in the flowering of Spanish Scholasticism as best represented by the great thinker, Francis Suarez (1548– 1617). However, this peak of Scholastic thinking can be viewed as hardly commensurate at all with the general tenor of the Southern Renaissance, especially ascentered on Italy. Indeed, one may see in this steadfast movement of scholasticism a muscular continuation of medieval scholasticism as if the Renaissance—and also the Reformation—had hardly changed anything. Part of this resilience, if we so describe this phenomenon, was because Iberia, both Spain and Portugal, had only been very lightly touched by these hugely influential movements which had deeply affected much of the rest of Europe.

Moreover, not only was scholasticism in Spain during this period vibrant, so too was mysticism in Spain, with the likes of Teresa de Avila, St. John of the Cross, and Ignatius of Loyola forming a coterie of mystics having few rivals to this day. Part of their impetus was certainly cast in the motivation of the Counter Reformation to make for reform in the Catholic Church after the onslaught of Protestantism. However, some of the impetus found in Iberia at this time must also surely be estimated as consequence of the overall strength of the Spanish Empire at this juncture. Indeed, there was more, for this is the age of some of the greatest Spanish literature, bathed in the language flourish of Baroque.

During some of this time, the Spanish Catholic Empire virtually stood at the front of the line of Catholic nations. Though often in competition with its smaller neighbor Portugal, (and from 1580 to 1640 assuming ownership of Portugal), both nations ventured into new and previously unknown parts of the world, taking Catholic ideology and institutions and missionaries on forays both east and west. Thus, in some fashion the optimism and the forward looking possibilities presented by the Renaissance somehow found parallel in this massive extension of Spain. To many Europeans the Spanish Empire in the sixteenth century seemingly stood at the forefront of the future.

Meanwhile, a studious Jesuit, Francis Suarez, alluded to earlier and belonging to a Catholic religious order intent to bring its lost Catholic population back from Protestantism, the Jesuits, found time to interact with the notable Renaissance thinkers Marsilius Ficino (1433– 1499) and Pico della Mirandola (1463– 1494). Therefore, Iberian Scholasticism was cognizant of veins of thought coming from the more well-known Renaissance of Italy. The aforementioned thinkers, both Platonists of a sort, are two peaks of Southern Renaissance philosophy.

Pico's treatise entitled *Oration on the Dignity of Man* is typical Renaissance writing in style and in content. However, the work is difficult to understand without some knowledge of Kabbalah, the knowledge of which a Jewish scribe had provided to Pico. In another published work, entitled *Conclusions*, Pico manifests his intent to achieve mystical union with God, which might be said to be his overall intention in his writings. Nevertheless, Pico's work has and somewhat remains outside any philosophical tradition of note, for his directives are couched in highly esoteric explanations hardly matched in likeness to anything before or after him. In this, nevertheless, Pico exhibits the wandering spirit so typical of some Renaissance figures. Hardly afraid of raising ire over his ideas with provocative language, he was censured by the Church.

The work of Marsilio Ficino represents also something of the eclectic sensibilities of Renaissance thinkers. Though an affirming Platonist, mixed in his thinking are strands of Stoicism and Epicureanism. As the Platonist, and in relationship with the famous Cosimo de 'Medici, he was one stimulus behind the newfound Platonic Academy in Florence. Of particular note with Ficino was his belief that religious belief was central to the human; in him we find no rather common though often muted Renaissance secular leanings. Moreover, he seems to think that philosophy, particularly Platonic philosophy, can partner with Christian thought and living to effect a salutary life. At the same time, he felt the receding religious beliefs among some of his contemporaries of high station compelled him to his self-perceived function as an educator. In this, his was a never-ceasing effect to present a way of living commendable to his peers who seemed to be losing their way.

When we come to Suarez in Catholic Spain, we also find some novelty, if not of content, certainly of form. That is, he is one of the thinkers who transitions from writing in the traditional medieval form of commentary and instead opts for an essay or treatise. This newer form of writing will catch hold and maintain itself in modernity. By contrast, and indicative of what might be called Suarez's old world attitude, is the fact that no revolutionary Baconian propensities for asserting the practical purposes of knowledge are detectable in Suarez. He upholds Aristotle's vindication of knowledge for the sake of knowledge as strongly as did medieval thinkers. Standing in the Thomistic tradition of Catholic philosophy he is perhaps seen as the last of the great Catholic scholastic thinkers who thinks in terms of the large picture of things, without, however, superseding or displacing Thomas Aquinas. Interestingly enough, Suarez's most popular work, *Disputationes meaphysicae*, was used in many Protestant universities for almost two centuries.

However much the Scholastic Renaissance differed from the larger Renaissance, both shared interest in the subject of political philosophy. That is, aside from the obvious name of Machiavelli, a name permanently attached to the Italian Renaissance, there are other notable philosophers such as Hugo Grotius and Jean Bodin writing on this subject. Within the Scholastic Renaissance, there is a comparable interest by Robert Bellarmine, but figuring most prominently is Suarez. Interestingly enough, both Bellarmine and Suarez argue against the theory of the divine right of kings, prominent at the time. In this theory, the king's justification of his position as sovereign issues directly from God. Obviously in such a form of political covenant, the power of the king is virtually invincible. However, Suarez argues against such a theory, and presents argument that the community of the governed, with their

81

consent, permits the sovereign to be their sovereign. As modern as this theory sounds to us today, it nevertheless has even older historical roots coming out of the high Middle Ages, to which Bellarmine and Suarez and other thinkers knowingly appeal. Obviously, such a theory was not the favorite of kings who were trying to hold onto the theory of their divine right to rule. This is why Suarez wrote his 1613 work, *In Defense of the Catholic Faith*, in opposition to the position of King James I of England. In the same year, James responded by having Suarez's book publicly burned in front of St. Paul's Cathedral in London.

Scholasticism, though with some changes, would continue to hold steady in Iberian geographical regions. By contrast, the Italian Renaissance seems overloaded with a myriad of philosophies, many of them revivals and continuations of classical schools, such as Stoics, Skeptics, Epicureans, Platonists, and Aristotelians and a smorgasbord of eclectics. In part because of a rising tendency of looking at the world through a scientific lens, another group of thinkers or seers arose who mixed together science and mysticism. Among them are some names still mentioned, such as Paracelsus and Jacob Boehme. To some real degree, the plethora of a large mix of philosophical orientations and doctrines was partly due to varied efforts at trying to combine something of an old way with new ways of thinking. Thinkers hardly thought of their efforts in this overt manner, but only a cursory look at some philosophies of the Renaissance evidences such mixtures. One must not forget that attempts like that in alchemy hung on for a long time into the modern period in the European mind.

As already mentioned, one set of new steps in political philosophy during this time is most evident in the political thought of Machiavelli (1469– 1527). Political governance is for him built around the maintenance of power; ruling a people concerns the maintenance of power with the means available. There is little to no moralizing in him and no "higher ends" to which the political state or political leaders should aspire. Appearance is as important as, indeed on many occasions more important than, realities. Sometimes from appearances, realities can be made; attention to the former should be paid for purposes of the latter. Often depicted as a pragmatist without principles there is in Machiavelli's political thinking concessions that are frightenly realistic about human nature. Machiavelli certainly represents a high point of Renaissance thought, but he is scarcely ever presented as a hero of new thinking; rather he is deemed as a savant of sorts in presenting a political world to come and is usually given little applause. In this sense his thinking is blandly prophetic for the future, though hardly hopeful. Machiavelli instructs his prince how to manage his affairs so as to be left standing at the end of the day. For him, metaphysical explanations or justifications for political action need not be attached to morals; indeed, in some ways, Machiavelli is a political positivist. That is, all the laborious work of justifying political law and rules from prior thinkers is dispensed with as simply unneeded with reference to political governance.

4. B. *Philosophy of Northern Europe*

The Renaissance concentration upon classical languages and texts provides one link from it to the opening of the Protestant Reformation. Like Renaissance thinkers desiring original texts, Reformation thinkers desired an authentic biblical text that was not corrupted nor haphazardly mistranslated. For the religious thinkers of the Reformation this most often meant the original Greek of the Christian New Testament and in 1516 Erasmus of Rotterdam, Holland (1466– 1536), published a Greek edition of the New Testament along with a new Latin translation. The very next year, 1517, Martin Luther posted his infamous document, Ninety-Five Theses, on a church door in Wittenberg, Germany. Within a year of each other, these two events were some of the latest harbingers from over two centuries of rumblings for religious reforms. With the crisis eventually known as the Protestant Reformation, this event permanently rips into two parts the previously and largely unified Christendom of the Middle Ages.

Though Erasmus and Luther never met they exchanged a number of letters, had a written disputation between them, but by the end, were trading insults against one another. Desiderius Erasmus as a Renaissance scholar and humanist was hugely interested in keeping the peace and this hope required the Church to put itself in order, both in head and members. Erasmus's humanism therefore tended to follow an ethical route that saw proper religion and proper religious practices as contributing to that end. In almost no manner, however, was Erasmus leaning in consciously secular directions. Rather, Erasmus was a loyal Catholic, but despised medieval philosophy and many medieval expressions of religion. He was a severe critic of abuses in the Church of his day, and some historians have contended that Luther only hatched the egg that Erasmus laid with earlier and stinging criticisms of the Church. Despite his aversion to philosophy and the repugnant intellectualization of the Christian religion, Erasmus nevertheless advocated a religious life and practice that is heavily indebted to his platonic leanings. For example, he thought that many religious externals, such as rituals, pilgrimages, relics, and rosaries, were not only unimportant for the religious life, but could be positively harmful. Erasmus advocated the cleaning up of religious life, and of the religious house of Rome. A strong emphasis upon positive ethical behavior and practice followed from his humanistic leanings. A tendency to place the heart, and not the head, at the center of proper religious life was at his urging. He was not, however, anti-intellectual. Nonetheless Erasmus would have supported the adage of Thomas Kempis (c. 1380– 1471) in one of the most read books of the age, *The Imitation of Christ*, that "I would rather feel contrition than know how to define it."

For Erasmus the philosophers had made the simple, complex, and wandered around any point to be made in a circuitous and fruitless fashion. On theological doctrines, Erasmus was insistent that not a few of the doctrines suggested in Scripture were beyond the ken of any elaborate human understanding. While Erasmus was certainly no agnostic in religion, he does resemble certain of the skeptics who show up during the Renaissance and early modernity, such as Michel Montaigne (1533– 1592). That being said, the business of real religion for Erasmus in his day was not so much painstaking and unprofitable thinking, but doing. This meant putting one's religious life in order, and for the officials of the Church to set the example in that effort. Most of Erasmus's notable works concern precisely this effort, with some being written with a biting satire that spared few, even renegade popes of the past, such as found in Erasmus's hugely popular *Praise of Folly*. The flavor of the book suggests that Erasmus is writing from the perspective of a Renaissance humanist who is bending down to aid a Church and Christian life which have fallen off of its own track. As critical as Erasmus was of the reigning Church, however, for most of his life no Church official dared to rein in or discipline the great man, no matter how stinging his indictments of certain churchmen. In great part his safety issued from his reputation: as the greatest intellectual of the time, to infringe upon his work would have met with all sorts of outcry and resistance from his supporters. Nonetheless, everyone has his season; favor toward Erasmus did not extend to the end of his life. By 1531 judging eyes gave warnings of caution to those reading Erasmus and works that had been vaunted as valuable works previously were placed on the Catholic Index. That is, these were works forbidden for the faithful to read.

85

In Erasmus's conception philosophy proper would provide little real gain to the religious life, and though Luther and other Protestant Reformers agreed, the agreement on this point masked deep underlying differences between Erasmus's preferred reform of the Church and the Protestant critique of Luther. At the same time, both men preferred reading the Bible and the Church Fathers to the medieval philosophers. However, Erasmus's Platonism (which Luther had branded "spiritualism" in his once theological partner Andreas Karlstadt) was abhorrent to Luther. More fundamentally, however, Luther contended that Erasmus's path to reform would be of no real effect. In Luther's estimation, almost all previous reformers of the Church had tried to clean up the life of the church, thus their overriding attention to morals. Luther in addition claimed that the doctrine of the Church was at fault. Therefore, two houses were needful of being put in order.

On the matter of salvation Luther and Erasmus raged their bitterest theological difference, with Luther contending that no vestige of human freedom could spiritually revive the human after the inundation of the Cosmic Fall. Save for the unmerited grace and love of God in Christ extended to humans, no human had anything at all to put forward toward the imitation of Christ. This Lutheran understanding of the human condition raised the whole issue of freedom and determinism, but also the issue of how reason and philosophy fitted into theology. While Erasmus desired to preserve the freedom of humans in the debate, Luther desired to preserve the freedom of God. Thus, Erasmus argued that in the discussion of the human– divine relation, fundamentally broken or not, it must nevertheless be the case that "God must be good," or do the right thing, to which Luther responded with "Let God be God." Despite his aversion to philosophy per se, Erasmus still held that reason had to be satisfied with theological truth and explanation, while Luther tended to separate and segregate God's work from human reason.

Luther is famous for his reference to reason as the "whore," and in uttering it may have sounded like Tertullian, but in his most famous defense before his Catholic accusers he notably appeals both to Scripture and to reason as the ground from which his accusers must articulate their disagreement with him.

Luther did desire to see philosophy extricated from the Christian theological enterprise, and was astounded that so much of the substructure of medieval philosophy purporting to be Christian had nevertheless used the thought and philosophy of a man, Aristotle, born three centuries before Christ and the Christian Church. Luther does not think Aristotle stupid for having been a philosopher, but Luther saw the Greek's thought as simply impertinent to the domain of Christian theology. Whereas Erasmus like Luther had an affinity for the Church Fathers, and of course, Scripture, Luther nevertheless cared little for Erasmus's proclivities for classical thinkers. Luther's successor, Phillip Melanchthon, however, will have more affinity to the previous scholastic thinkers, for many of whom Luther saw little pertinence to Christian thinking. It is Melanchthon and his school who will continue to use some of the works of Catholic scholastics, such as Suarez in Protestant schools. Luther, by contrast, held up a figure like Bernard of Clairvaux as a previous medieval thinker worthy of study. Bernard, it will be remembered, was a stinging critic of scholastic thinking.

Erasmus did not bear his dislike for medieval philosophy alone. In great part because of the perceived stuffiness and logical but unnecessary subtleties concerning minutia of medieval thinking, many others stood poised to revive the humanistic emphasis of Renaissance thinkers finding new thinking about the human in the study of classical thinking. Not far behind this new appetite, moreover, was a mechanical device—the printing press—that would add speed to the intellectual torrents of the time. Indeed, alongside the many reasons that can account for the

Protestant Reformation, the printing press is near the top. Now pamphlets and books could be duplicated with astonishing speed, compared to the old way of slow scribal hand-copying.

The popular satire of Erasmus would soon find other satirists, like the Frenchman Francois Rabelais (1494– 1553), who would present the bawdy along with the uplifting, and who would start to suggest that perhaps toleration should have a larger role to play in religious squabbles than it had been allowed in the past or in the present. Of course this theme was reminiscent of Erasmus and writers like the Englishman Sir Thomas More (1478– 1535), who would start to conceive of a world overcoming the vicissitudes of their world, as found in More's *Utopia*. These visionaries were therefore necessarily staunch critics of past mistaken practices, and not just with religion. Before long educational methods and formats—chief among them the repulsive Scholasticism—would be treated unmercifully, as it was in Rabelais. These men and their criticisms were just the beginning, however, for new conceptions of knowledge and therefore teaching were surfacing. Hosts of competing theories about most everything began to swirl in this new world, spurred by the Renaissance and the Reformation.

Not surprisingly, in this morass of sorts, skepticism again began to raise its head. Perhaps the greatest skeptic of the time, the Frenchman Miguel Montaigne, would make doubt seem humane and eminently practical. While his own country of France was suffering immensely from the antagonisms of mainly Catholic France with Protestant Frenchmen, Montaigne encouraged a suspension of beliefs since they could hardly be justified with any certainty, even at the bar of reason. Urbane and witty, Montaigne provided a picture of a civilized nation and person who could maintain his finessed composure under a variety of difficulties, to include not having the last word on much of anything. Completely unlike the rustic and solitary Egyptian monks of the desert from over a millennia earlier, Montaigne's stylized person is in command of himself, without being in command of virtually any final knowledge. With Montaigne's conception of what a human should be like, we see something of a Socratic reversal. That is, whereas Socrates spread his questions over Athens and waited to challenge any hopeful but probably naïve answer, Montaigne suggest that challenge of this kind demands simply too much of limited human knowledge. That is, we need to get used to not knowing, for we can be comfortable with it and should be, for final truth is too far away from us for any to make claim to it.

Just as the Spanish Empire in only a few decades previous had appeared to stand before Europe as the supreme power, so too now an island and previously backwater nation, England, began in the latter sixteen century to emerge as a noteworthy competitor among its neighbors. Furthermore, having largely and successfully managed to create its own nation church under the authority of its own monarch, rather than under the superintendence of the Bishop of Rome or Pope, the confidence of the nation to go its own way elsewhere surely seemed possible to some. An independent streak would soon prevail. At first intimidated by the much larger power of Spain, the infamous defeat of the naval Spanish Armada in 1588 gave the English confidence and the Spaniards pause for a season. Meanwhile, like the earlier sea ventures of the Spanish and Portuguese, English ships set sail for distant lands and would in time establish a network of colonies in the new world, rivaling the Iberians on land, and not just at sea.

By the late sixteenth century, an English Renaissance was unmistakably underway in this small country, and the names of its notables are names known to the world to this day—Thomas More, William Shakespeare, Francis Bacon, Inigo Jones, and John Donne, to name but a few. Bacon, moreover, in terms of changing the direction and intent of knowledge, would direct the way into modernity.

4. C. Philosophy of Francis Bacon

The disaffections of a string of Renaissance, Reformation, and particularly early modern thinkers for the prior Scholasticism is evident in Erasmus, Descartes, Hobbes, Locke, and others, but none are perhaps so notable and so virulent as the critiques of the English thinker, Francis Bacon (1561–1626). The time required a thinker providing viable direction for a bright future. That future was gleaming evident in the production of William Shakespeare's plays and the voyages and discoveries of Cabot, Drake, Raleigh, and others. Furthermore, while not yet quite firm, an English settlement at Jamestown in the New World was beginning. Out of all of this, what Bacon anticipated—but his age was hardly making advance toward—was a method for ensuring steady successes for the future in the realm of science. Bacon, moreover, had his work cut out for him, because in his estimation the educational and university establishment was sunk in a past view of the world and a wrong view of knowledge. If ever there was a thinker prepared to catalog the errors of the past and make a plan for the future, it was Francis Bacon.

Bacon came from a very notable family of East Anglia in England. Though Bacon was living in a time defined from the past, as are most all ages, Bacon appears as noticeably ready to move beyond the world of his forbearers. Though practically still a youngster at a mere sixteen years of age, Bacon gained admission to Gray's Inn, after having entered Cambridge at age twelve. Bacon's father Nicholas had been Lord Keeper of the Great Seal for Queen Elizabeth I, and Francis would follow him in a political career spurred by ambition.

Bacon not only rose through the political ranks of the day from the House of Lords to Solicitor-General and culminating in Lord Chancellor. During the same period of occupying some of his offices, he managed to commit to print portions of his project of changing the conception of knowledge, and most importantly, its capture. Unlike the fate of Boethius about a millennium earlier, Bacon did not suffer irreparably when he was dismissed from the office of Lord Chancellor for illicitly taking gifts. He was, however, prohibited from assuming political office for the remainder of his life. Nevertheless, in hindsight this may have enabled him to do more of what his previous political work had constrained. The previous politician could turn to philosophy and science.

Bacon believed the times needed to change, and in nothing quite as much as the quest for and the purpose for which we pursue human knowledge. He was not areligious or a secularizer in that regard, but what is most striking in him was that he was blistering with his attacks on past philosophy and its ineptness. The essence of Bacon's project was to in effect remove the perceived prior encumbrances of the speculative excesses. These issued from the philosopher, but needed to be reined in by the disciplined work of science. That is to say, Bacon thought it practical and useful to work around and without a constraining conceptual apparatus constructing by philosophers from eons ago, particularly that of Aristotle. The metaphysically charged terminology of "substance" and "essence" and other such like terms, for example, obstructed the path to knowledge according to Bacon. Much of the debate from the past and the philosophy and science of his day consisted of quibbling with mere words, Bacon charged. Bacon believed quibbling over such terms provided no advances in knowledge advantageous to other than a philosopher enamored of his presumed skills in abstract thinking.

Most important historically was Bacon's charge that the purpose of knowledge was in its utility or practical application. That is to say, it is in the practical benefits of something known that we find the reason for having pursued knowledge at all. Many of the philosophers of the past, however, addicted as they were and are to useless finessing of definitions of "substance" and like terminology, advanced real knowledge not an inch. Indeed, in this prior conception, the philosopher was one who stood above and prized knowledge for the sake of knowledge. Bacon wanted knowledge for the purpose of life and living. Knowledge needed to be brought to earth, so to speak.

Naturally, with the clout of Aristotle's science still in vogue among many in Bacon's day, Bacon would have to swim against the stream. But so had Copernicus and Galileo and a host of others, who had insisted that undue respect for Aristotle's philosophy had and was even now impeding advances in science. Aristotle, therefore, became something of Bacon's greatest enemy. Bacon's paragraphs often provide occasions for the new man Bacon to call out the old man Aristotle, and to force the latter to admit that in terms of practical benefits to humanity that Aristotle had provided, Aristotle has given little to the point of next to nothing. Aristotle has given to the philosopher something that only the philosopher could value, whereas what Bacon is urging in his scientific enterprise is the kind of knowledge that will offset the merciless dominance of nature over humanity.

On the point of methodology, Bacon contends that pursuit of knowledge in the past had proved sterile by the unfruitful exercise of attempting to deduce knowledge. Underneath this tendency of excessive reliance upon deductive thinking was the ubiquitous reliance upon mathematics. These considerations push Bacon in the direction of empiricism, or to more accurately describe Bacon's conceptions, experimentalism and experience. Unlike the form of Descartes or Leibniz's philosophy, Bacon will not esteem the mathematical model or method as the magical elixir for eliciting further knowledge. While Bacon has been criticized for his perhaps exaggerated harshness toward both mathematics and the deductive method—as both are often required by science—his criticism is pointed toward an excessive reliance upon both.

Moreover, and in defense of Bacon, the early modern realization that mathematics could be

pivotal to unlocking some knowledge of the world also partially contributed to the tendency to

believe knowledge could be determined almost alone by simply logic, in the manner of

mathematics and deductive method. We see something of this perhaps most with the famous

rationalist, Barach Spinoza (1632–1677). Therefore, the realization that most of our knowledge

is accessed through experience of the world, that is, testing and experiment, takes some time to

catch hold.

Given the practical nature of Bacon's notion of the purpose of acquired knowledge, it

almost necessarily follows that knowledge of metaphysical matters is pushed to the periphery

and rather obviously deemed as unnecessary to the point and reason of scientific inquiry. In such

a manner, Bacon is opposed to maintaining allegiance to the notion of final causes in the

Aristotelian account of causality and science. While not subscribing to a later notion of the

fortuitousness of events, the attribution of final causes to events in nature produces no beneficial

knowledge to the inquirer or to scientific investigation. Furthermore, while not rejecting

theology as an admitted field of legitimate study, for Bacon the field of scientific study is the

world of material being; the world of spiritual being has no place in the study of science proper.

The realm of the immaterial and the spiritual do not have the necessary materiality so as to be

made fit objects of scientific study. Such ideas are rather strikingly like those of the English

thinker Thomas Hobbes (1588–1679), excepting for the fact that Hobbes, unlike Bacon, is

content to draw deterministic conclusions from scientific study, and more willingly associated

with possible atheism than Bacon.

Bacon is of course most known to persons outside the field of philosophy for his pithy saying that "knowledge is power." Indeed, much of the orientation of Bacon's philosophy is condensed within this sparse but extremely influential string of words. Extrapolating upon them enables one to see how precisely commonsensical Bacon's meaning is to a Western culture of modernity having considerably enshrined Bacon's main ideas as they concern knowledge. One might even say that while the philosophers in general have been the harshest critics of Bacon, lay persons remain his greatest applauders, however little or much they are acquainted with the facets of the man and his writings.

At worst, Bacon can be bemoaned as providing illicit credibility to modern consumerism. That is, if the goal of knowledge is to bring knowledge and know-how into the service of humans, then such intent in time produces a culture where the satisfactions of humans are served by a scientific knowledge making possible satisfactions of those human desires. The human community therefore takes presumed control of itself by taking control of the means of knowledge that science makes possible, and the rest, we might say, is history. However insufficient as a comprehensive "philosophy of life" the dictum that "knowledge is power" is, the critic who charges Bacon with making possible an excessively consumeristic culture is making an anachronistic charge. That is, one is doing historical violence to the thinking of a man if we conceive of him as thinking of modern luxuries now on the horizon. Instead, he is thinking of extending, for example, the lifespan of modern lives. In Bacon's day, this would have been, at best, around two-thirds of the number of years we Westerner's live today.

In other words, one needs to consider that Bacon's thoughts on knowledge are significantly built around his motivation to alleviate some of the hardships and tragedies of human life. This is the reason why he bends the purpose of knowledge in the direction of aiding humans in their plight in the world. In this context, Bacon's death at the hands of pneumonia after catching cold from stuffing a dead chicken with snow becomes understandable; the man was considering the beneficial effects of cold surroundings on meats that perish quickly at room temperature. Domination of nature is not for the purpose of taking our presumed rightful position as the highest of all beings. Dominion over the world of nature demands that we have knowledge of it. From this knowledge we can manipulate the world in which we find ourselves such that we have reasonable chance of surviving into adulthood, and having reached that, living a few more years beyond.

On the other hand, with a philosophy so focused upon the material world and the difficulties of living within it, the spiritual aspects of life, though not the intention of Bacon, may be compromised, if not perhaps totally set aside or diminished. While Bacon's ideas might not be significantly placed in such a category of consequences, it is worth noting that a corrective is certainly capable of swinging too far in another direction.

Chapter 5
Early Modern Philosophy

5. A. *The Birthing of Modern Science and Modern Philosophy*

Modern philosophy begins with Descartes (1596–1650), often called the "Father of Modern Philosophy." The rise of modern philosophy commencing with Descartes is paralleled with and causally intertwined with the rise of modern science. For philosophers of this time, this means philosophy is formulated as thinking reflecting on the new scientific conceptions of the day. Conflicts were sometimes inevitable. In the case of Immanuel Kant (1724–1804), for example, he fears that the scientific conceptions of Isaac Newton (1642–1727) and others may render human morality spurious by explanations submerging and possibly eradicating the previous place for human freedom of action. Unless human persons are truly free in their moral decisions and actions then moral responsibility is without meaning, contends Kant. George Berkeley (1685–1753) writing a half-century before Kant, had undertaken to prove that the material world was not immovable as the foundation of reality. Berkeley took this stance fearing that the implications of scientific materialism would impugn the existence of God who was immaterial. In these and other examples, we witness the impact of the new conception of the world from modern science upon philosophy.

A little noticed fact about Descartes is that this frequently touted "Father of Modern Philosophy" was also a soldier during a portion of the Wars of Religion, a time of bloody events usually associated with a time more religious than the time of Descartes. Because of the confluence of events around the times of change, we can expect to encounter individuals and whole movements that sometimes straddle markers of our historical devising. Descartes, it might be said, lived in one world, but wrote himself into the next one. Though it rarely happens that historical changes come so suddenly, the turn from medieval to modern philosophy is perhaps one of those rare moments in human history, glimpsed through the life of Descartes.

Modern philosophy, however, did not come without some invitations from the past. The previous Renaissance had provoked a time of exploration and experiment, even though the Renaissance largely looks backward toward the past. In looking at the past, however, some Renaissance scientists and philosophies became reacquainted with the atomistic theory of Democritus (c. 460–360 BC), for example, which pushed inquiry into new (but also resuming old) directions. Renaissance thinkers wanted to return to a revered classical world for their philosophical models after rejecting prior philosophical legacies of the medieval period, like the philosophy of Thomas Aquinas. Renaissance philosophy, however, becomes more than simply looking further backward, to Plato or to Aristotle, for example. Indeed, the increasingly impugned science of Aristotle now comes under intense scrutiny, not to say eventual and almost total rejection in the early modern period. The seeds of the scientific thinking of modernity will sprout and prove deeper challenges to the prior medieval philosophy than had the philosophy of Aristotle for Christian medieval thinkers in the High Middle Ages.

With the Renaissance return to classical models, there are revivals of classical Stoicism and Skepticism among Renaissance philosophers. As earlier mentioned, among the most prominent of these is the Frenchman Michel Montaigne, who delighted in highlighting the conundrums of thought that stymied the best thinkers. Descartes himself is oftentimes wrongly seen as a skeptic, when in fact he desired certainty against a renewed assault on reason by skeptics. The reason for deeming Descartes skeptical is that he combats skepticism with skepticism and thus very much looks the part of a skeptic. This method is part of his ploy to show the contradictory nature of excessive skepticism. Proceeding to doubt everything, he says that when he is done he cannot doubt that he is doubting and ultimately this leads to his famous quip "I think, therefore I am." From the prior doubt, Descartes proceeds to reestablish the reality of most of the ordinary world. In so doing, Descartes gives a new rationalistic stance to philosophy, where "clear and distinct ideas" are insisted upon.

Because the influence of religion is still strong, however, the thoughts of philosophers are often tempered by religious considerations to include the thought of Descartes. Typically even the skeptic, after casting doubt on human knowledge, would proceed to claim knowledge provided by God through faith to mitigate the previously admitted skepticism about human knowledge. On the other hand, with the increasing focus of the Renaissance on the world of nature and the material world, art and science will tend to eventually give less attention to spiritual matters. The popularity of mysticism during this period also partly issues from an absorbing study and contemplation of nature. Pantheism, a belief that God is not only present in the material world, but in some sense is the material world, is pronounced in some of these thinkers. In 1600, a former Dominican monk, Giordano Bruno (1548–1600), was deemed a heretic and executed by the Roman Inquisition. Bruno, who despised the philosophy of Aristotle and who was receptive to the new Copernican theory of heliocentrism, found his way toward a pantheism that put him on notice to the Church authorities.

The desire to emulate the classical world by the Renaissance was matched by the desire of Reformation thinkers for authentic texts and manuscripts of the Bible. Many of the conglomerate of these individuals became extraordinary linguists of classical and koine Greek in their effort to uncover the original writings of the classical world and the early Christian Church.

At the same time, more and more thinkers started to write and make translations into their national tongue, such as English, French, or German, rather than the previous universal Latin of Western Europe.

The religious controversies spurred by the Reformation would continue in theological circles and break out among nation-states as the so-called Wars of Religion. Some philosophers began to theorize more independence for political entities in the contest of power with the papacy, for example. Perhaps most startling from this period and serving as a portend for the future are the assertions of Machiavelli who advises that a political ruler not be weighed down by moral rules, and who permits himself to tell falsehoods to his citizens if the falsehoods advance the interests of the state. By the time political philosophy comes to Thomas Hobbes (1588–1679) and then to John Locke (1632–1704), the philosophy of government had evolved to the point that the desire for some element of self-rule by political subjects starts to find a theory.

It was a scientist and mathematician, Blaise Pascal (1623–1662), who as a contemporary of Descartes, opposed some directions of rationalist thought, by charging that Descartes renders and depicts God, for example, as the "god of the philosophers." His meaning is that Descartes's rationalist approach to some subject matter distorts its subject. Furthermore, though Descartes is consciously Catholic, Pascal sees Descartes philosophizing in a way that however inadvertently minimizes the philosopher's religious belief. For Pascal, Descartes is a philosopher who happens to be a Catholic, rather than a Catholic philosopher. Pascal indicates his own stance toward reason with his statement that "the heart has reasons which reason knows nothing of." With this statement, Pascal is contending that the philosopher is erroneously presuming an exclusive avenue for knowledge and even knowledge of God—cerebral reason. As is evident in the controversy between these two thinkers, questions of epistemology are increasingly occupying early modern philosophers.

Descartes had other critics, like Hobbes, who saw Descartes as trying to avoid the implications of the new scientific way of looking at the world. Whereas Pascal saw Descartes as going too far in his philosophy, Hobbes sees Descartes as not going far enough. Hobbes declared that an incorporeal substance (like God) made no sense, and that God would have to be corporeal to be a fit object of study. Moreover, Hobbes was less concerned with God than with matter and saw no reason to explain anything without reference to bodies in motion. Thus, unlike Descartes who had sought to preserve an immaterial component of the human person to safeguard human free will, Hobbes implicates all reality as made up of matter. From this materialism, Hobbes stands ready to accept the resultant determinism that Descartes had fought and which Immanuel Kant (1724–1804) will go to sophisticated lengths to avoid. The issue remains a perennial one for philosophers to this day.

Much of Hobbes's resulting metaphysic will become rather popular, though at a later time, in contrast to scientific efforts of the sixteenth and seventeenth centuries. In these centuries, with Hobbes as notable exception, most thinkers are content to accept the scientific investigation of the world and religious beliefs as somehow compatible. Their increasing understanding of the complexity of the world made undeniable to them the laudable genius of the Designer who made such an intricate world. Something of this association is evident in the statement of Galileo (1564–1642) that God wrote (or made) the universe in mathematical pattern. This kind of symmetry implied to such scientists a reasoning and reasonable God whose creation could be penetrated by understanding, even if merely by finite minds probing the mind of the Infinite through the creation. This association, however, will start to weaken in subsequent decades as the world and the human for that matter are increasingly seen as autonomous and described in separation from God. Certainly part of that distance from deity is marked by an earlier hesitation, even by the Englishman scientist Isaac Newton, to refrain from formulating "final causes" in the way that Aristotle had done.

5. B. *Philosophy Coupled with Epistemology*

Descartes, as the "Father of Modern Philosophy," highlights a philosophical tradition within modernity of acute effort to resolve questions about human knowledge. Descartes is followed by Spinoza (1632–1677) and then Leibniz (1646–1716). Collectively these three philosophers constitute the crux of a tradition we call Continental Rationalism. The reference to rationalism and rationalists here is to the epistemology and the epistemological views of these thinkers. Philosophers with such a label believe that the mind has primacy with regard to knowledge, and that there exists certain ideas which are innate to the human mind. This means that these ideas, however few, are independent of any knowledge that might derive from the human senses.

Rationalism as a theory of epistemology had a long history among philosophers before modernity and is perhaps best represented by Plato. Like most labels, individual "rationalists" nevertheless exhibit variant forms of rationalism. Plato, as example, is a firm rationalist who is a recollectionist regarding knowledge. The latter term means that he holds that the human mind possesses all knowledge, though as the human person plummeted from the world of Forms to the earth in Plato's cosmology, they forgot what they once knew. Because the forgotten knowledge is buried deeply in the mind, recognition of its presence requires a skillful teacher such as Socrates to raise the buried knowledge to the light of day and thus to conscious awareness.

Modern rationalists have tended not to be recollectionists, by emphasizing more the role of reason or intellect in the production of knowledge as opposed to the senses. Likewise, very few rationalists are quite as ardent as Plato to absolutely shield knowledge from the debilitations of the error-prone senses, though cautions are voiced about the dubious nature of the senses compared to the discerning mind. Such rationalists, therefore, do not go so far as to deny any role of the senses of sight, sound, taste, touch, and smell in producing knowledge. The mind screens the data of the senses, while coordinating the production of human knowledge.

For the empiricist, also with a philosophical history as old as that of rationalism, and represented by Aristotle and others both before and after him, the rival rationalist conception of the mind and senses is essentially reversed. That is, the mind produces no knowledge without the influx of the senses and without that contribution, there would be no knowledge at all. The rationalist and the empiricist are thus explaining the same thing—human knowledge—but with different viewpoints on how such knowledge is formed. The rationalist is obviously not going to contend that pieces of historical knowledge, like the year the American Civil War ended, can be conjured out of an unschooled mind. On the other hand, the rationalist will contend that unlike that example, there is some knowledge we have which is resident in the mind and without the aid of the senses. This means that we know these things independently of the world of our senses. Examples would be the belief that something cannot both be and not be at the same time. Another example would be the belief that the distinction of judgment between more and less is innate to the human person. Locke, as disagreeing empiricist, denies the validity of both examples.

These two positions, rationalism and empiricism, therefore, are acutely poised in opposition, but when we come later to visit Kant's epistemology, we will see that he attempts to couple the strong points of each position while weeding out the weak or wrong contentions of each. The epistemological tradition of British Empiricism (as opposed to Continental Rationalism) derives in particular from opposition to the rationalist notion of innate ideas. Here John Locke is followed by George Berkeley (1685–1753) and finally David Hume (1711–1776). Locke is famous for his empiricist contention that the mind is a *tabula rasa*, or blank slate. St. Thomas, as another empiricist before Locke, had affirmed that there is nothing in the mind that is not first in the senses. These statements mean that the mind is analogous to a platform or stage that must wait for the set and players to position themselves on it before a play can begin. There is no play (knowledge) until the set and players (contributed by the senses) are brought to the stage. Locke is likewise insistent that nothing can be known in the human mind until this happens. Locke offers, as examples vindicating empiricism, that it is impossible to imagine a taste one has never tasted, or that a person born blind could identify colors on the first exposure to them after surgery giving him newfound sight.

The empiricist point of view, properly understood, strongly implies that any notion of the possible or impossible is meaningless prior to experience. That is, if I have no acquaintance or experience with animals, nor have been given any information about them from other persons or sources, I would not know what animals would be capable or incapable of doing—driving a car for instance. It is only after some experience of animals that I could formulate a notion or concept of what animals are and are not capable of, at least in some general way. At the same time, for empiricism to be true, every piece of knowledge or idea must be traceable to or accounted for by the contribution of the senses to the mind. Even our most complex ideas must derive from the senses and even ideas we might deem so primordial—like the distinctions of more and less.

David Hume (1711– 1776) put empiricism to acute test on this very point. Hume is generally counted an empiricist but also a skeptic of sorts, for he contends that empiricism cannot account for all of human knowledge, but he does not retreat to rationalism in the end. The specific notion he scrutinized was the origin of our idea of cause and effect. His claim is that no experience of our senses provides the source for the belief that one thing is the cause of another. Hume's explanation for the belief we nonetheless have is that we have a habit or custom of drawing the inference that one thing causes another simply because we observe them in constant association or union or, as he says, in "constant conjunction." We never, according to Hume, actually observe one thing causing another. However, if this is true, then empiricism is flawed as a theory of the source of all of our knowledge, because it claims that all of our ideas are derivative from the data of our senses. Hume contends that his example shows that this is not so.

Following on the heels of the Renaissance and the Reformation, as earlier indicated, skepticism had begun to flourish again, and in the search for "real" knowledge, epistemological investigation began in earnest in early modernity. This obsession of modernity, if we may call it such, is to produce an account of the origin and justification of human knowledge. In the world of the philosophers of early modernity it is noticeable that the aforementioned modern rationalists and empiricists are most known and still read for their epistemological views, despite the fact that most of them wrote on other philosophical subjects. Hume, for example, wrote on ethics and Leibniz on metaphysics and Locke on political philosophy.

Looking backward on the epistemological debates of these significant philosophers, and to be joined by Kant also, we can surmise with the insight of hindsight that these thinkers were struggling against an old and long tradition concerning knowledge. That tradition had tended to source knowledge as issuing from the reading of authoritative texts and discussion of the intricacies of meaning, often with scant regard for evidence of the type we would now consider essential to a definitive decision. To some degree, moreover, the early modern realization that mathematics could be pivotal to unlocking some of the prior mysteries of the world, though hugely advancing knowledge in some of the sciences, nonetheless also partially contributed to the already popular tendency to believe knowledge could be determined almost alone by deductive inference, in the manner of mathematics and deductive method.

The realization will be historically slow in coming that most of our knowledge must be acquired through experience of the world, that is, testing and experiment, and that strong and even reasoned thinking and deduction are not exclusive or guaranteed avenues to know much of what we place in the category of knowledge today. An example from Plato's work entitled Meno will illustrate the mixed results of the deductive aspiration, in light of Plato's ardent version of epistemological rationalism. In that dialogue Socrates guides a young unschooled boy toward a geometrical problem that Socrates contends the boy will be able to solve with some direction from Socrates, but without Socrates providing the answer. True to Socrates's claim, the boy comes to the right answer by a series of logical deductions the boy makes under the guidance of the probing questions given him by Socrates. It is Plato's contention from such example that this kind of realistic and true experience proves that the boy knew the answer before he later came to realization of knowing the answer.

As many critics have pointed out, however, there are other and very many questions Socrates could have asked the boy in which the lad would undeniably require a matter-of-fact investigation by him or someone else in order to arrive at a correct answer. A logical analysis alone and by itself, therefore, would fail with such questions. An example that would exhibit this limitation of deductive knowledge would be to ask the boy how many planets are in our solar system. No amount of deduction alone could arrive at the correct answer to such a question. With such example, then, many have contended that in general, empiricism seems substantially correct in its assertion that the parameters of our knowledge are constrained by our acquaintance and experience with the phenomena in the world. The rationalist, however, would contend that unmediated sense experience alone is insufficient for knowledge without a mind programmed to give form to the raw material of the senses.

5. C. The Romantic Reaction against the Philosophy of the Enlightenment

If early modern philosophy (until about 1800) is characterized by focus upon epistemology, the nineteenth century is an age of moral and social philosophy, and permeated by the prior and strong reaction of Romanticism to the excessive rationalism of the eighteenth century. Many Romantic thinkers, like Jean Jacques Rousseau (1712– 1778), for example, are repulsed by the mechanistic images of the universe and the human person advanced by prior thinkers. Romantics will advocate human lives more in tune with nature and lived with spontaneity and without the hypocritical pretenses of social station in society. Rousseau famously contends that "Man was born free, but is everywhere in chains," while sympathizers of Romanticism will contend that much of past Western history bears out their thesis.

This attitude, or philosophy, which appears to opponents to favor a retreat rather than an advancement of knowledge or society, rather naturally provoked mocking. As an instance of this, Voltaire (1694– 1778) writes to Rousseau to complain that having walked on two limbs for the whole of his adult life, he will find it difficult to return to all fours. Nevertheless, Rousseau contends that modern civilization has soiled and imprisoned humans, while advocating return to a primitivism that will reinvigorate something of a "noble savage." Such humans possessed an authentic character lacking in an artificial and contrived modernity. Nineteenth-century thinkers will charge the prior two centuries as having introduced a maelstrom of problems by forcing the human out of his natural habitat and natural habits.

A frequent contention among Romantics was that their thesis could explain some previous conundrums of human history. For example, and according to the Romantics, bafflement over why the once powerful Roman Empire fell was simply because that "civilization" had veered too far from nature, something that its invaders, the "barbarians," possessed in abundance. The American Transcendentalist Thoreau (1817– 1862) will pen the sentence that "In wilderness is the salvation of the world," and this at a time historically when men were subjugating nature to their own small and selfish purposes. If the human wanted to be nurtured in humanity, he needed to be closer to nature than numbing cities permitted.

Though Romanticism's attack on the rationalism of the Enlightenment was most severe in the age of the eighteenth-century Enlightenment, the influence of Romanticism extends well beyond that century. As example, the social philosophy of the nineteenth century in many ways is a Romantic response to the Industrial Revolution. Similarly, Kant's philosophy was a response to the Scientific Revolution wedded to his sympathies with Romanticism and particularly to Rousseau. Indeed, Kant's philosophy, for all the influence of the prior rationalists and empiricists, is indebted perhaps most to Rousseau—a fact often ignored in descriptions of Kant's philosophy. Also with Romantic underpinnings, Karl Marx in the nineteenth century attempted to return the economic life to the natural rhythms of working humans, for human life had been turned topsy-turvy by free-market economies brought on by an Industrial Revolution that played havoc with human anthropology. A whole gamut of societal ills had made human life miserable according to such critics and their attempt will be to right a world gone badly wrong. It is no small wonder that the Romantic reaction to the Enlightenment is often labeled the "Counter Enlightenment."

In one way of portraying the history of humankind, antagonism between rationalism and Romanticism serves to highlight variant emphases of thinkers concerning the nature of the world and humans within that world. Just as to some degree epistemological empiricism arose as a criticism of epistemological rationalism, so too in Romanticism arises a significant criticism of the logical, measured, and mathematical emphases latent in a modern rationalism and so often joined to science. Parried down to reveal a greater antagonism between the two positions, one might contend that rationalism gives deference to mathematics and facts in pursuit of reality, while Romanticism opts for fancy, fiction, and feeling to produce contentment. Indicative of the power of Romanticism over some of the philosophers mentioned in this book, moreover, is the fact that some of them, though supremely known for their rigorous and logical minds, admitted, indeed experienced, the lure and reality of Romantic feeling within themselves.

The life of the great philosopher Plato is illustrative of the conflict that these two emphasis can sometimes evoke within an individual. The story goes that having observed Socrates as an extraordinary philosopher and teacher, Plato went to the great man and asked to be his student. The astute Socrates, noting that Plato was at that point in his young life something of a poet, presented Plato with a needed and required choice between poetry and philosophy before Socrates would take him on as a student. Plato consented to choose philosophy over the competition, but the beauty of the writing of Plato's *Dialogues* is testament to the fact that the poet within could not totally be quiet. The often quoted phrase from Plato's Dialogue *The Republic*, about the "ancient quarrel between poetry and philosophy," thus found example in one of the greatest rationalists of all time. Some of this rationalism is evident in Plato in his notoriously severe comments upon art and artists, which and who are very often allied with Romantic inclinations. Aristotle, who is not nearly as critical of art or artists as Plato, at the same time makes the pertinent assertion that poetry is more philosophical than history, because history is about the particular, while poetry rises to the level of the universal. In this estimation, poetry would be akin to philosophy in a way not commonly noticed—except perhaps to a romantically inclined individual.

These brief remarks reveal something of the depth of the romantic inclination and perhaps enough to account for some of the animosity of Romanticism for the excessive perceived rationalism of modernity, and particularly the rational excesses of the Enlightenment. However much Enlightenment figures were swooned by and virtually idolized the promise of the new and advancing scientific interpretation of the world to produce blueprints for advancing humanity, their Romantic critics were only too ready to point out what a protractor or a measuring instrument missed in describing a human. To these Romantic critics, a pernicious reductionism was assumed when, for example, an Enlightenment figure such as Pierre Cabinis (1757– 1808) asserted that "the brain secretes thought as the liver secrets bile." The inherent grossness of such a perspective had, to the critic, missed entirely what was the essential human. The smugness of the reductionist mentality was loathed by the Romantic, for the Enlightenment had made the human being and the world they lived in appear to be like machines when neither were.

Moreover, the strong optimism that was a characteristic trademark of Enlightenment thinking following on the heels of scientific progress would now confront the sobering possibility that science might produce a map of the world and the human resulting in a feared determinism. In other words, the possible inevitability of knowledge that Kant so feared now

seemed a real liability with the new science. With such a possible result, some observers might

prefer ignorance. In fact, not a few of the Romantics openly made such a claim. At the same

time, this kind of reaction to the new knowledge provoked the applauders of the new sciences to

dismiss their critics as simply burying their heads in ignorance of the world and the future.

Rationalists saw themselves as making prior mysteries and religious faith defunct and therefore

obsolete. The Enlightenment, in other words, was in part unmasking the beliefs of the past for an

expectant optimism about the future.

However, if the new knowledge initially produced an optimism it could in fact also

produce hesitation—as can be seen in Kant—but there were other worries. Of course not all

thinkers, philosophers and otherwise, were either rationalists or Romantics exclusively. Some,

like the Frenchman Voltaire, had shades of both. The perception by Voltaire that some things

that might be true might nevertheless not be beneficial to society, caused him to depart from

fellow Enlightenment thinkers that presumed the ordinary man would have to learn to live with

reality, whatever intellect and science determined it to be. However, one of his contentions was

that even if God did not exist (Voltaire presumed not to know), it would be, in his words,

"necessary to invent Him." Voltaire considered that this religious belief did not exist in

abeyance from the fact that many if not most people regulated their moral behavior in light of a

perceived judging God. If belief in that God were removed, this could also, and likely would,

provoke moral indifference on the part of the prior believer in God. Better to keep the belief,

even if untrue to reality, Voltaire reasoned. Realism, therefore, might have to take some license

with the truth. Enlightenment optimism would have to be tempered with some concessions to ordinary human nature. Such a concession to human reality, moreover, had already been

asserted by the Romantics against the rationalists.

Chapter 6
Immanuel Kant and His Critics

6. A. The Philosophical System of Kant

Immanuel Kant (1724–1804) is one of the greatest of Western philosophers. Kant came from humble circumstances, his father being a saddler and the household of his youth was permeated by German Pietism, a Christian theological tradition emphasizing Christian living and doing of good works, and for the most part shunning formal theological knowledge as unnecessary if not injurious to the proper Christian life. Kant himself could be described as religious to some degree, but his philosophical orientation, when considered as a whole, much more reflects values of the European Enlightenment and less residue of a religious past. Nevertheless, there is something of a religious thread observable in Kant's philosophy, even as his thinking consists of modifications of some prior religious ideas. As positive example, after presenting hallmark critiques against the validity of arguments for the existence of God, Kant does give some measure of approval to the moral argument for God's existence. As negative example, in his book *Religion within the Bounds of Reason*, he rejects the notion of a substitutionary atonement as found in orthodox Christian theology.

Kant in many ways is a thinker not so much looking toward the past for resources, but rather trying to chart the course forward and he presents something of the optimism characteristic of Enlightenment thinkers in his writings. Kant is also something of a late bloomer. His infamous *Critique of Pure Reason* was written when he was fifty seven years old, though the works that follow come in relatively quick succession. As often recounted about him, he never went outside his native Prussia, though he had amazing geographical knowledge. He was meticulous with the schedule he kept. His afternoon walk was so punctual that households in the neighborhood checked their timepieces by sight of him walking.

Kant's philosophy can be placed within the debates over epistemology evident in his philosophical predecessors, from Descartes to Hume. Kant's contribution to that debate lies in his effort to combine both empiricism and rationalism into one epistemological theory, rather than choosing one over the other. The merits of his epistemological theory are still debated among philosophers who often refer to epistemology before and after Kant, as indication of the quality of his work. In this work, metaphysics for the most part receives a thrashing, reflecting the fact that metaphysics and epistemology are inextricable tied together in Kant.

Kant had been an epistemological rationalist until he read the writings of Hume. His reading of Hume, however, did not turn him into an overnight empiricist, but did spur him to consider how parts of rationalism and parts of empiricism might be fused together. A larger issue looming in Kant's mind, however, was not only the internal philosophical debate between empiricists and rationalists, but Kant's worry that the mechanistic world revealed by the Scientific Revolution and the ethical world of humans were different worlds. In fact, each seemed to exclude the other. That is, the problem in Kant's mind came by considering that the discerned laws of the universe discovered by science suggested that the world was determined in its movements and actions. Simply said, the world of matter followed the laws governing matter. That world thus becomes predictable with the discovery that this world works in accordance with laws which dictate its behavior. The human world and the humans that populate it, however, presumed that freedom was present for them in a way in which it was not resident in the rest of nature. Kant, therefore, saw his task as seeking to reconcile these two worlds, whereby wecould have science, and whereby we could also have a freedom necessary to make sense of human morality, which nevertheless seemed not to be a component of the world from the perspective of science. The world of science was an amoral world; the world of the human was a moral world. Any reconciliation in Kant is predicated on his admitted assumption that we presume a freedom of action in human subjects that we cannot vindicate, indeed have reason to doubt, from the perspective of science. Nevertheless, because we cannot be sure that deterministic conclusions concerning human subjects are in fact true, we presume that we do have human freedom, when in fact we have no such certain knowledge. Living life without such a presumption would make for a confusion of our moral lives.

For Kant's rapprochement between rationalism and empiricism his solution is a hybrid epistemology in which he agrees with the empiricist that all of our knowledge begins with the experience of the senses. However, he also agrees with the rationalist that not all of our knowledge arises from experience. This means that for Kant there is a structure to the human mind that makes the information supplied by the senses intelligible. He agrees with the empiricist that until some sense data is brought to the mind there can be no knowledge, but he agrees with the rationalist that sense data not processed by an organizing mind would produce no knowledge. This organizational template is provided by categories of the human mind that funnel the incoming data from the senses in accordance with the structure of the mind. In effect, all human knowledge is conditioned or qualified by these components or categories of the human mind.

Kant then asks a question which impacts upon his view of metaphysics, or more precisely, upon the possibility of possessing a true knowledge of what is ultimately real. (From what has been indicated thus far, the reader can likely surmise Kant's answer.) That question is what is the relation of the categories of the mind to the thing that the mind is focused on? Asked another way, does the way we understand reality (with the categories of our mind) correspond to reality? Is there a match, so to speak? Kant's answer to this question is simply to say that he does not know and he can see no way in which this could be known. Therefore, Kant is a metaphysical agnostic. This means that what the knower knows about reality is what his mind configures from the sense data provided, but he can never know if what the mind tells him it is, is what it actually is. Kant's philosophy, then, draws a negative conclusion for metaphysical matters. He blunts this negative conclusion, however, by having in effect two philosophies; he has a theoretical philosophy and a practical philosophy. The latter is one that is necessary so as to make sense of much of human life by relying upon notions like freedom, which are called into serious question by Kant's theoretical philosophy.

In ethics, Kant's name is virtually synonymous with deontologism or duty ethics. Kant's version of what is ethically correct or right is frequently deemed too rigorous or rigid by many readers. This is because Kant is something of a moral absolutist. That is, if something is right, it is always right and vice versa. This absolutism is corollary to Kant's refusal to take account of any consequence which might pressure a decision maker to divert from what is absolutely the right thing to do. In other words, for Kant the right thing to do is the right thing to do, irrespective of consequences, either positive or negative. Ethics, therefore, imposes duties and responsibilities upon us, from which we cannot deviate by circumstances we might consider sufficient to allow us to circumvent those duties. The problem with consideration of consequences for Kant is that they allow decision makers to bend the rules, by placing the rules at the mercy of consequences. Kant will have none of this and therefore in his estimation a lie and stealing are acts to always be forbidden. This is true in even the most dire and potentially fatal situations.

It is nevertheless too easy and largely a mistake to simply deem Kant's philosophy of ethics bereft of the presumed mercy of considering consequences to allow for some latitude in decision making. That is, though refusing to allow consideration of consequences in ethical decision making, Kant's ultimate appeal is paradoxically something like an appeal to consequences. In other words, it is for the reason of the consequences in the world of telling a lie, that I should not lie. Moreover, if one's adherence to telling the truth is so pliable (because we deem consequences pertinent) that after a while, we almost expect people under pressure to not tell the truth, the ultimate trust we place in people is weakened. In this ultimate weakening of truth telling, the bonds that hold things together soften and are capable of a collapse sufficient to bring down the whole house. Better to take the pressure and follow the rule even when the decision to do so hurts. Thus, one can see that Kant's appeal is to something like universalism. That is, for the sake of the larger group or society, I should not allow myself to exempt myself from moral rules that I am all in favor of everyone else keeping. Though this may be and often is very painful to do, it is necessary to do, Kant thinks. The critic might persists by asking if there is nonetheless ever any price to be evaluated as simply too high or costly in order to tell the truth? Kant would say no, but would also insist, in line with his argument so far, that the evident pain and suffering possibly avoided by allowing consideration of huge consequences is largely ephemeral. That is, the pain and suffering avoided in not keeping the rules in some extraordinary instances, will have the consequent deleterious effect of making our suspicions stronger against someone who may actually be telling the truth. A lie, therefore, may work, but does so simply by stealing from the credibility of truth, when it pretends to be something true, when it in fact is

117

not. In this way one can see that excessive deviations from truth in time will diminish even the capacity of a lie to masquerade as truth. This is because our commitment to truth telling is rightly under suspicion by too many deviations. A lie therefore takes away—like a thief—from the hand that feeds it.

Kant's way of thinking about ethics nevertheless exudes the fact that he sees the human as an autonomous creature. That is, the individual should be in charge of his own person and not relegate that responsibility to someone else. Kant's philosophy therefore reflects something of the "man coming of age" mentality, prominent in the age of the Enlightenment. This is why Kant advocates that the moral system of the individual be one in which we are governed by morals which are "self-legislated." This does not mean subjectivism or relativism, but that we abide by the rules we do because we believe and affirm their cogency, and not, as a consequentialist might, because someone else tells us to, or we fear infractions may produce dire judgments. In a truly moral person for Kant, there would be no requirement or need for a policeman or God to enforce right morals. Furthermore, true goodness in a person requires that that goodness comes forward freely in any action, and without calculating consequences prompting the goodness. If one derives gain from their presumed moral act, then they are not truly acting morally, only ultimately selfishly or at least with calculating prudence. This is why Kant famously wrote that the only human good that is good without qualification is a "good will." He means by this that our intent or motivation in an action is only truly categorized as good or moral when the desire to give something to another, for example, is only and solely motivated by the intention of giving. This is to say, again, without consideration of any possible consequences deriving from our action.

6. B. *The Philosophical System of Hegel*

Hegel is one philosopher often spoken of with great opprobrium by philosophers of today. Indeed, the general dismissiveness with which the name of Hegel elicits negative response necessitates some historical background for such disdain. Though Hegel's philosophy is steeped in metaphysics, that fact only begins to account for some portion of the dislike of a thinker immensely popular not only in his day, but for decades afterward. Hegel is an idealist and the belief of idealists that mind is responsible for and in some way commensurate with reality, rather than matter, hardly sits well within a culture of philosophers today who are more prone to opt for materialism. Given how common this belief is today among contemporary thinkers—and also not infrequently by ordinary people living in contemporary society—the negative attitude toward a philosopher such as Hegel pointing in the other direction is hardly surprising.

As already indicated, the reception of Hegel's philosophy in his own day was immensely different. The rather astonishing success of Hegel's philosophy during his day and for close to a century afterward also needs some historical explanation, as Kant's infamous critiques of reason might seem to have effectively silenced or doomed any future effort to undertake metaphysics. With Kant's contention that human epistemology does not allow the human mind to glimpse the ultimate markers of reality, Hegel's explanation of what reality is would seem at first sight in deliberate ignorance or indifference to Kant's critiques. In fact, however, Hegel contended that Kant's pronouncements on epistemology and by implication metaphysics were hugely flawed. Kant made two mistakes which Hegel put to use for his own philosophy.

While drawing attention to the human perception of reality as structured and conditioned by our mind, Kant's account suggests, on the one hand, the possibility of the mind as in effect

119

substantially creating reality. That is, the structure of the mind would seem to force "reality" into the mold of the mind. It would seem then that the mind has not only a significant hand in the manufacturing of reality, but is the driver of the entire process. Indeed, Kant himself implies something like this when he refers to his position as analogous to a Copernican revolution, though in epistemology, not cosmology. By this analogy he reverses the traditional epistemological explanation of his predecessors. They had presumed that the mind adjusts itself to the reality it encounters and thus provides an accurate picture of it. Kant, however, contends that the mind does not adjust itself to reality; rather, reality is adjusted by the mind. The predominance of the subject person in this position is evident. That is, the constraints upon knowledge are imposed by a subject working within the context of his mind while presuming objects and things outside the mind.

Hegel pounced on the implication of such a position and pushed it in the idealist direction where we might say, mind creates (or at least implicates) matter or the world. That is, it now looks as if we might contend that the knowing subject in some fashion constitutes the objective reality of the world. The prominence given to the structure of the mind in Kant's account of the formation of human knowledge enables Hegel to contend that mind is reality. Hegel, however, was not finished with Kant yet. Kant's metaphysical agnosticism had forced upon Kant some stipulations that Kant's epistemology simply could not bear, according to Hegel. Chief among these were Kant's reference to an "Unknown X" to designate the presumed things and objects of which the human mind forms and extracts knowledge. Hegel perceptively contended that Kant's meager epistemology of unknowing provides him with no warrant for any such bold claim. In effect, therefore, knowledge is beholden to the mind and not some presumed objects far afield and independent of the mind. The debate over knowledge is thus recast by Hegel in a revised metaphysical account tightly woven into epistemology. Starting with his two criticisms of Kant, Hegel was able to bring the human mind to real knowledge of itself or reality, or what Hegel calls the Absolute. One might say additionally that the psychological twist of Kant's epistemology is still present in Hegel's epistemology, though in Hegel it is much stronger, and unlike Kant, not at the expense of not knowing about an unknown world.

Beyond the legacy and criticisms of Hegel's account of metaphysics, Hegel has prestige and some following among philosophers working in the camp of the philosophy of history. Hegel's theory about the workings of history is usually condensed as one in which a thesis encounters an antithesis, with the result being a synthesis that is the result of that interaction or altercation. In Hegel's mind this is how historical transitions, indeed all of history, happen. In this fact, history shows its supreme importance, simply because it is history that conditions how and what we know. In this Hegel shows his divergence from Kant, who thought knowledge was constrained by mind, whereas Hegel thinks mind is both constrained and augmented by its historical dimensions. One might even say of Hegel's philosophy that whereas the centerpiece of Kant's philosophy is epistemology (and by association, metaphysics), the centerpiece of Hegel's philosophy is history (and by association, metaphysics).

With Hegel's emphasis on attention to history, it is not surprising that he takes considerable interest in the history of thinking and not only philosophy. His historical account of philosophy similarly goes beyond bare interest in the historical account and elevates the historical understanding of philosophers to something of a metaphysical underlining. That is, the history of philosophy is not the mere recounting of various and conflicting philosophical viewpoints, but it is also illustrative of the path of self-realization or knowledge that comes into fruition as discernable metaphysical pathways. In this way historical knowledge is the complement of metaphysical knowledge, culminating in absolute knowledge of the Absolute. Hegel thus gives importance to thought and the cumulative effort of thought by philosophers. The result will be an ultimate and unifying philosophy composed of what was once, but erroneously thought of previously, as so many disparate or contradictory philosophical streams of Western thought.

Somewhat like Aristotle who conceived that thinking was the defining feature of the human species and the philosophers the most acute thinkers of humanity, Hegel similarly gives priority to the philosophers for continuing to make clearer a truth that had been captive to previous states of human consciousness and history. Historically human art and religion have presented truth, but these incomplete forms, while persisting in culture today, recede in importance as the illuminations of philosophy unmask clouded and previous markers toward truth, culminating in what Hegel thinks of as the witnessing of ultimate knowledge as well as freedom.

The unfolding of this freedom is the unfolding of truth, known as the Absolute. That Absolute is something of a conglomerate or synthesis of subject and object. Seen rightly, as the philosophical mode of consciousness makes possible, the human knowledge of this Absolute is not only self-knowledge, but also the Absolute knowing itself through the human subject. The human in this depiction is not flaunting hubris by treading on any forbidden territory (the Absolute or Divine). This is because the Absolute comes to know itself in us, because we are something of the means by which Thought thinks itself.

For a philosopher who emphasizes freedom as much as Hegel, he has paradoxically been charged with the opposite by his presumed glorification of the state. Such criticism to a degree is simply unfounded because while Hegel sees the individual state as embodying individual freedom, he does not support an authoritarian state whose business it is to subjugate or force obedience upon its citizens. One might say that in Hegel the state makes possible the ultimate realization of the capabilities of the human individual. Interestingly, Hegel, and very different than Kant on this point, believed individual states to exercise sovereignty, such that no state should be forced to submit to another state by sheer exercise of the will of one domineering state—or union of states— opposed to another. States must seek the welfare of the people in their state; the state therefore should never compromise its own will and freedom to another state, so as to endanger the welfare and security of its own people. The final court of appeal for such a dispute may require force of arms, and Hegel concedes the point from Heraclitus that "war is the father of us all."

In his philosophy of history, and tied in with his political philosophy, Hegel infamously makes reference to the "end of history." By this phrase Hegel means not that history or time will stop, but rather that the final realization of human freedom found within the state will afford humans unprecedented opportunities presented in what amounts to democracy. The procedures and policies of such a state provide therefore what individuals have universally worked toward. In other words, with the goal within reach, the desired self-realization is made possible by a political system providing the means to do so. The end of history does not mean a state of human stagnation begins when history ends, but rather that the realization of human desires as exhibited in such a democratic state will not be superseded by one better, for there is not one. The goal of history is precisely this state of human realization, afforded by a regimen no longer compromising the human spirit by placing one human at the behest of another, as found in the practice of human slavery, for example.

In Hegel's philosophy of right (essentially philosophy of law), he has justified claim to an idea for which he is given scant credit or attention today. Hegel's notion is that the growth of a society is in some sense a function of what he calls a "struggle for recognition." What he means by this, commensurate with his critical estimation of human slavery, is that true human freedom only actually occurs when one's claim to freedom is real to the point of being admitted by another or others. In other words, if the society in which we live truly affirms us as free individuals, then we are free indeed. Thus, for Hegel there is a required link between the individual and society, such that in the absence of a society which in some sense legitimizes the individual, the individual lacks something essential, something required. This is in great part why the human is a social being, for the requirement of freedom for the individual requires a society which acknowledges that on the part of the individual. The modern idea of autonomy, so dear to Kant and men of the Enlightenment, is affirmed by Hegel, but within the struggles of a social context necessary for its affirmation. Hegel fills out the particulars of his idea concerning recognition within his famous master and slave dialectic, to indicate the unsuitableness of this relationship in a truly free society. A society structured upon the kind of domination present in the master– slave relationship is ultimately one portending vicious struggle. No resolution will come until the identity of the master is no longer bought with the price of another human living in subservience to him. This will not occur until the two parties manifest recognition of the other as an equal. In this fashion, Hegel's philosophy of the state can hardly be called authoritarian.

Chapter 7
Nineteenth-Century Philosophy

7. A. Mill, Nietzsche, Marx

During the 19th century the continuing influence of the English moral tradition with Francis Hutcheson (1694– 1746), David Hume (1711– 1776), and Adam Smith (1723– 1790) struck a new cord in the moral philosophy of Jeremy Bentham (1748– 1832) and John Stuart Mill (1806– 1873). The net effect of these two thinkers upon ethical and social thought is the broadening of idea of liberty. Mill, for example, argued for the emancipation of women in his *On Liberty* in 1859 and against what he referred to as the "tyranny of the majority" in a democracy. Earlier, Bentham connected his utilitarian moral philosophy to practical and governmental reform in England. Largely because of the work of Bentham, the Reform Bill of 1832 passed the English Parliament. The Bill was introduced by Bertrand Russell's grandfather in 1832, Lord John Russell (1792– 1878). Victoria would become Queen of Britain and Ireland five years later, in 1837.

While Kant had taken the position that right motive or intent (or will) is the judge of what is good moral choice, the utilitarianism of Bentham and Mill argued on the opposite end. The British utilitarians contended that the perceived consequences of moral choice should make the judgment of whether the moral choice is good or bad. The consequences one should aim for are pleasurable or happy consequences. The avoidance of consequences that are painful and produce unhappiness follows. What made this moral philosophy appealing was that it appeared to disciples that people as a matter of fact operated like utilitarians when they made any choice, moral or otherwise. That is to say, every choice persons make is made with the hope of realizing some goal that one desires. One never, for example, desires pain for the sake of pain. People will, however, endure pain for the sake of pleasure. Furthermore, even if one finds pain pleasurable, the utilitarian still finds confirmation, in that though this distorted sense of pleasure is hardly one shared by most others, it still counts as pleasurable to the one pursuing it. This objective, therefore, is the reason he pursues it, however unfathomable to most others.

The complaint against utilitarianism was that utilitarianism used morals for something different from morality by its suggestion that happiness was the proper goal of moral decision. Opponents maintained that the two were often different. The complaint against utilitarianism was that we sometimes make moral decisions that we believe to be right, but that are also painful and costly to us. Right moral actions therefore sometimes produce great grief and unhappiness.

Mill, however, is convinced that utilitarianism is the underlayment of any moral theory, to include even a religious ethic. He thus writes: "In the golden rule of Jesus of Nazareth, we read the complete spirit of the ethics of utility. To do as you would be done by, and to love your neighbor as yourself, constitute the ideal perfection of utilitarian morality." Though Mill as a utilitarian contends that pleasure and happiness are the goals of moral choice, his ethic is increasingly cast by him as one that fulfills human nature. In other words, utilitarianism does not so much serve at the behest of pleasure and the avoidance of pain, but as an ethic that directs humans toward their duty. This sense of duty is certainly implied in Mill's famous statement that "It is better to be a Socrates satisfied, than a pig satisfied." Pleasure and pain here are certainly at some remove from right and wrong, and Mill, by such an admission, would not seem to be utilitarianism's strongest advocate anymore.

Frederick Nietzsche (1844– 1900), the German thinker and author of such provocative titles and readings as found in his *Genealogy of Morals* and *Beyond Good and Evil*, will manifest little but disdain for the utilitarian tradition in moral philosophy, and most particularly for Mill. Nietzsche's thoughts on morality too exhibit a turn toward consideration of the unconscious with respect to the springboard of human action, anticipating Freud's work in the next century. Nietzsche's analysis of Mill finds fault with the utilitarian for only studying the conscious aspects of resultant behavior. Nietzsche wishes to go deeper and, indeed, further back to survey and evaluate the various anthropologies evident in the history of Western man.

As is evident in comparison to Nietzsche's philosophy, Mill's philosophy stands at the head of much nineteenth-century optimism and charts a continuing course for Western civilization indicative of better things to come. At the same time, we might say that Mill and Nietzsche's philosophy represents two variant streams of secular thinking in this century. Mill sees brighter things on the horizon, while Nietzsche, and though with some sense of positive expectation, sees something of portending collapse of the cultural past of the West. Much of this collapse, in not atypical fashion, Nietzsche welcomes, but he is too much of a realist to suggest that out of the ashes may come something better, though such is possible. From Nietzsche, moreover, there is an explicit call to turn back and away from the Christian and Platonic tradition in thinking. Nietzsche protests against a tradition of philosophy in which philosophers simply polished the thought of their predecessors. Nietzsche calls for philosophers to be like artists— real creators. Nietzsche likewise has some of his harshest criticisms for philosophers because they are more obedient than they are original. Nietzsche, therefore, is a relentless critic of traditional morality, arguing that it is the morality of slaves because it presents the highest moral value as that of obedience. From this despicable past, people should chart another course.

In contrast to Mill, Nietzsche argues that people have a fundamental will-to-power that manifests itself in their moral choices. Thus, Nietzsche replaces Mill's idea of a universal human desire for happiness and pleasure with a universal need of will-to-power. According to Nietzsche, Socrates manifested this desire to climb on top of Athenian society when he appears to most to be only asking innocent questions, such as what is virtue or what is knowledge. Nietzsche therefore has a view of the human personality or psyche in which all people, even slaves, have this need and will use every means to wrestle power away from persons lording over them. Nietzsche, moreover, because he prizes individuality, is suspicious of any mass movements, to include democracy, because he places the greatest possibilities at the feet of the greatest individual, called the *Ubermensch* or superman. Nietzsche's favorite work and one providing a sketch of Nietzsche's plan for the future is his *Thus Spake Zarathustra*. In it he also details his fears that the society of his day is so peopled with lackadaisical human weaklings that perhaps no supermen are among their pathetic numbers. Though some thinkers were beginning to notice the writings of Nietzsche before his death in 1900, his books have been increasingly popular since. He might be counted one of the half dozen most read philosophers of our day.

Karl Marx (1818– 1883) is certainly one of the most influential philosophers of modernity. In great part this is because Marx studied and charted a social revolution that to some degree was absorbed in the political revolutions that transpired in the twentieth century in Russia in 1917 and China in 1949. In his own day Marx's views only threatened the status quo in Europe, but the ideas provoked enough notice so as to make Marx's political radicalism feared in European capitals at the time. Not without warrant, then, did Marx speak in the opening sentence from his famous *Communist Manifesto* that "A spectre is haunting Europe and that spectre is communism." There had been communists of a sort before Marx, but it was this German who gave the idea a good deal of theoretical and practical explanations that are still studied and argued in our day. The old communist regime as found in the former Soviet Union may be dead, and the "Free-Market Capitalism with Socialist Characters" may be a concession to the death of old-style communist thinking in China, but that being said, the number of Marxists in the world today is by no means negligible.

To set much of the stage for enunciating Marx's philosophy, we must begin with the Industrial Revolution, which in many ways was the offspring and one consequence of the previous Scientific Revolution. The real possibilities that emerged from the Scientific Revolution enabled the time of the Industrial Revolution to be termed rightly the Age of Machines. Generally speaking, we might say that much machine labor was substituted for previous hand labor, though at this stage and in most all cases, the resultant machine still required human labor to monitor it. Secondly, the burgeoning assembly line for production and manufacture of articles streamlined business operations and radically changed work environments. When operating as intended, these two facets of the Industrial Revolution resulted in a productivity light years ahead of previous centuries. However, as a result some unexpected consequences ensue and Marx proposed a theory to remedy them.

With unprecedented production of goods, overproduction of goods could now be a gigantic problem, with periods of unemployment becoming rather commonplace. From this observation and many others, Marx deduced that the capitalist economy was one that in time would self-destruct. Part of the reason for a calamitous end was the disgruntlement of workers having to endure the vicissitudes of market mechanisms wreaking havoc among the workers, or proletariat. Nevertheless, the promise of a better life enlisted workers to run machines and devices and the workers became part of a great migration from rural regions to cities where businesses and factories and therefore employment were most often located. Excepting for periods of overproduction and consequent lay-offs and unemployment, in the upsurge of markets, capitalist producers sorely needed workers. With the Industrial Revolution and the positioning of machines for production in cities, there were migrations from agrarian regions to these cities for work and the promise of a better life. This situation put the owner of the means of production, the capitalists, generally at great advantage, for great numbers of hopeful workers were seeking employment. Moreover, if workers are competing among themselves for jobs anytime workers outnumber jobs, then the rate of pay can decrease to the point of plummeting. The worker may therefore end up working for a pittance, and given how little he takes home with himself at the end of the day, he hardly has the means to walk off an excruciating and low-paying job. More importantly, because he has virtually no savings at all, he must return to work each day for he cannot afford to be sick or hurt. Therefore, he is in effect, something like a slave or serf. This is why Marx in the *Communist Manifesto*, at the very end asserts, "Workers of the world unite, you have nothing to lose but your chains." Chains, after all, are all they have.

As an alternative, Marx proposes that the workers themselves should own the means of production, in which case they would in effect be working for themselves rather than an unfeeling taskmaster. For Marx, the history of humanity had been precisely a history of prior conflicts and tensions between classes of people. His theory, however, offers possibilities for a "classless society." Indeed, in the class antagonisms of Marx's day, the worker experiences alienation because the conditions under which he lives and works force him to loathe his work. The contradiction is that, according to Marx, the human by nature is a worker, but the economic components of a capitalist society are forcing the worker into an unnatural work and cultural environment and pushing him toward the precipice of revolt. In communist society, by contrast, and to take but one example, the aggravating divisions of labor, so helpful and crucial for the speed and output of the assembly line, will be overturned. What will happen as a result, in Marx's famous words, are that one could "hunt in the morning, fish in the afternoon, rear cattle in the evening, criticise after dinner, just as I have a mind, without ever becoming hunter, fisherman, shepherd or critic." The world, or the human world of work that satisfies, will be restored. In such a scenario, the background of Romanticism is evident.

7. B. The Influx of Asian Thought

The Western World seemed remarkably unknowledgeable of things Asian for the most part until discoverers from the likes of Spain, Portugal, Holland, France, and England, some beginning in the late 1400s, made initial contacts with some foreign cultures. There were only a paucity of contacts of the West with the East prior to this time. Giovanni of Montecorvino, a Franciscan, had trekked to China in the late thirteenth century, and of course there is the fabled tale of Marco Polo (1254– 1324) the Italian making a famous visit there, also in the late thirteenth century. The Catholic religious order of the Jesuits were among the very first modern Europeans making entryway into China, Japan, and India, though starting only decades after the Council of Trent brought that religious order into being. From these men, moreover, we have some of the first trustworthy accounts of the new cultures and ideas encountered by these observant Westerners in the presence of things Asian. As knowledge of the world of the East became slowly but increasingly available, the future of idea exchange and influence looked promising on some fronts. As one example put to ideological use, the positive appraisal on the part of some French thinkers of the eighteenth-century Enlightenment was that within Chinese culture no

131

religion seemed evident. In the European search for a new age for humankind such news buttressed their stance that a society and culture without religion was not only preferable, but indeed empirically possible.

To place ourselves in the historical time period of the first Western visits to new shores, it is necessary to rethink a too brutal picture as the whole story of some of the details of first contacts. In Jamestown in 1607, in what would be the first successful English colony in the new world of North America, the receptivity of the native peoples to the newcomers was understandably guarded but in time became more relaxed, at least for a while. These newly arrived settlers were perceived as weak rather than the opposite. Observing that these gentlemen of an English sort had difficulty feeding themselves, the natives in all probability presumed no need to worry over these struggling newcomers. After all, not a few of them had come from a social class hardly acquainted with the sturdy requirements for sheer survival. Somewhat similar is the story and impression lent of the first modern encounter of the Chinese with the Europeans. A Portuguese boat had sauntered into a Chinese port in 1513 that would eventually become known as Macao. The arrival of the Portuguese ship, but more the appearance of the first sailors off the boat on which they had been a year, were not, to say the least, impressive to the Chinese. Looking more like ruffians than the cultivated and clean ambassadors the Chinese had assumed for such an occasion, the Chinese saw no reason whatsoever to be impressed or overwhelmed, much less envious of these pathetic human specimens.

Tragically, these peoples, both the native and half-clothed Americans and the cultivated and suave Chinese, had little indication of how much their lives and culture would be in the long term impacted by these encounters as successive waves of newcomers came to their shores. However, there is more complication to the story than the raw first encounters of cultures and strangers meeting face to face. The case of imperial China of the late eighteenth century illustrates just how miscalculating confidence could turn to tragedy, as it did in that great and ancient civilization in the subsequent two centuries. The details are simple. Something of the opulence of Chinese culture had been evident to Westerners for some time, and in 1792 the King of England, King George III, commissioned his envoy, George Macartney, to travel to China to attempt establishment of a trade agreement with the Chinese Emperor. The long and short of this story is that ambassador Macartney was unable to fulfill his mission, but after Macartney's return King George received a letter from the Emperor indicating that no trade deal such as the British King desired was feasible. This was because, as the Emperor expressed it, the English produced nothing that the Chinese wanted, much less needed. His people, the Emperor said, were contented people and had no need for such stuff as the English had to offer. The Chinese, in terms of this encounter, perceived themselves as strong enough to in effect ignore Western pressures, whether for trade or for something more. The Chinese presumed themselves to possess enough cultural capital to maintain themselves against potential adversaries. A few more decades would be required, in successive dealings with the British, for the Chinese to witness their mistaken estimation of these foreigners.

The previous cultural confidence of the Chinese would falter in time. By the end of the nineteenth century some Chinese intellectuals were casting about for ways to survive the onslaught of Western influence. In this context, some Chinese intellectuals began to express hostility toward the traditional Confucianism that had dominated China for centuries. Others gave specific attention to Western ideologies which had clearly given the West its dominant position in the world. Giving increasing attention to the thought of Karl Marx, in 1921 the first meeting of the Chinese Communist party took place in Shanghai, on the heels of the communist Russian Revolution of 1917. Significantly, the first prime minister of China after the office of Emperor of China was abolished, Sun Yat-Sen (1866– 1925), had received an education that introduced him to Western ideas. Sun, moreover, had expressed great frustration at some Chinese intellectuals refusing to consider various Western ideas. China now was in ferment, culminating in a civil war, climaxed by the victory of the Chinese Communists in 1949. Confucianism, previously the legacy of China for almost two millennia, was faulted for the backwardness of China in the twentieth century and for making a previous gigantic empire susceptible to the power of the Western powers. Westerners still studied the ancient religious and philosophical traditions of China, but Chinese intellectuals were now pouring over Western works to discern Western secrets.

The case of Japan's interaction with the Western world is fundamentally different in response, compared to the Chinese. Japan, like China earlier, had received a visit from the West, but this time, in 1853, the visitor was from America and named Commodore Perry (1794– 1858). His ship was loaded with gifts for the Japanese hosts upon arrival. Perry, however, told his hosts upon departure that he would return in one year with an empty ship and that the Japanese should be prepared to trade. High-level discussions and soul-searching began in earnest for Japan's future. The Japanese decided that the Western powers clearly possessed a superiority in the world and that it would be in Japanese interests to follow suit. From this decision would come a rejection of the Confucian heritage that had previously informed modern Japanese culture. There would also be rejection of the much revered order of Samurai that had once stood as the nation's first line of military defense, simply because critics charged that these warriors were simply outdated for success in modern warfare. With the charge to in effect, remake the nation, there would follow a period of increasing nationalism, embodied in the ideology of Shintoism that poised Japan by the time of the twentieth century to become an aggressor nation among its Asian neighbors. The West, moreover, took fundamental notice of this new power on the world stage, when, in 1905, the Japanese were the victors in the Russo-Japanese War. In 1937, Japan invaded an area of North China, an event sometimes calculated as the beginning of World War II.

Western penetration of India, virtually exclusively by the British, had begun when Queen Elizabeth I granted the East India Company a charter in 1600 for trading privileges within India. Commercial activity in time produced an enterprise in which the company became something of an autonomous and governing country within the subcontinent of India. The clout of this form of nation building and dependence upon India grew so substantially that in 1877 Queen Victoria was made "Empress of India," so as to concede something of the obvious. Though Victoria never physically visited India she was hugely interested in it, and not a few Englishmen had careers serving the Company. James Mill (1773– 1836), father of the philosopher John Stuart Mill, was one. The elder Mill was severely critical of Hindu culture in India, and argued for the legitimacy of British intervention in the sub-continent. An atheist himself, Mill could hardly be expected to have sympathies with the native Hinduism of Indian culture. Westerners not infrequently brought a rationalist perspective to such foreign shores, with the effect sometimes of weakening the native religious culture.

By the nineteenth century there was some increasing interest in Asian ideas by Westerners. However, this interest hardly issued from what we might call at the time mainstream philosophy. As example, Schopenhauer's metaphysical interest in the will prompts him to delve into the Hindu Upanishads for such material as he might find useful. Truth be told, however, Schopenhauer's nemesis Hegel makes not only significant allusion to some Asian ideas, particularly in aesthetics, but also in aspects of his writing on the history of thought in transition. However, Hegel, in comparison to Schopenhauer on things Asian is something of a Western triumphalist. That is, he thinks that Western and rational modes of thinking show their superiority to the competition in the ring of ideas. In other words, the Asian ideas are foils to something bigger (and by implication, better) than those ideas. Schopenhauer, who has no such idea, is looking in a sense for ideas noticeably different from Western ideas. Nietzsche, as another thinker spreading his interests far afield, had made significant allusions to Buddhism in his writing. However, Nietzsche is so full of irony and tease that while he appears to make some identification with some Buddhist ideas, real sympathies are difficult to establish. Though today Nietzsche is often deemed to be an apologist for nihilism, he does sometimes refer to that element in Buddhism, but most often as a negative judgment. Perhaps this is because Nietzsche at bottom proposes a philosophy that is life-affirming against all odds, and he perceives that Buddhism is indeed more than anything else, negatively nihilistic.

Certainly the element of the unconscious and the primordial, often found as ideas prominent in Hinduism, Buddhism, and to some degree Taoism, made these Asian ideas candidates for what some few Western thinkers were now turning toward. Certainly the Western tradition was remarkably insular prior to the early modern age, and while early modern contacts with other far afield cultures awakened some interest, it was more the case that when Western culture, speaking very generally, began in some part to tire of some of its own ideas, that it turned elsewhere.

However, we can make another kind of argument here. We might contend that Western attention to Eastern ideas, at least in philosophy, is because philosophy since Kant (and thus for over two centuries) has become so highly technical that lay interest in philosophy is quite and abnormally miniscule, not to say nearly impossible. If expertise in the discipline elevates aspects

of the technique of the philosopher so far above the lives and acumen of his reader, then the

reader searching for some answers may become restless. Here the East may look more attractive,

in part because of the differing teacher– learner relationship still found in the East.

Moreover, such an aid is sometimes necessary, as some of this religious/philosophical literature

is by no means easy to negotiate, and especially for a Western student.

As intimated earlier, the story of any initial convergences and meeting of the minds of

East and West is largely not exercised from the perspective of West looking East, but rather of

East looking West. Furthermore, the latter look is a consequence predominantly of Asian notice,

but not always of Western ideas per se, at least in the beginning, but more so of Western

hardware, with such things as weapons and armaments. By contrast, however few those drawn

to Asian culture in the nineteenth century from the side of the West, most were not looking for

any technology they might find in the East. Rather, they liked what we might call the

impractical ideas. One witnesses something of this appetite in the Romantic Movement and

particularly in American Transcendentalism. In this view, Taoism, as example, provides a view

of nature very unlike the Western Baconian view of nature as something to be subdued and

manipulated for human gain and benefit. The groundwork for East meets West is being created

in such small visions, but it will take another century before the fuller weighing of such ideas

will be undertaken with stringency and more seriousness.

7. C. Philosophy in Light of Science (Comte, Darwin, Spencer)

Auguste Comte (1798– 1857) is both a visionary of the future, though also a frequently

criticizedfigure in the philosophy of the nineteenth century. On the one hand, in moving toward and embracing the positivistic notion of science he articulates a notion of scientific explanation increasingly popular thereafter. However, his notion of a "religion of humanity" found few followers for the future. Indeed, he has been often mocked for his efforts, indicative of one modern and strenuous effort to further shed religious and theological components completely from science and philosophy. In the attempt to lend some understanding of Comte, we might suggest that Comte only wanted to capture some religious energies for science. If the religious element is just too religious for most, it seemed nevertheless that his hope was that science would assume the place and importance of religion of a prior age. Stated in this fashion, however, one can miss the subtlety in his understanding of the dynamics of a society that was previously religious. That is, his desire was that scientific society contribute to the cohesiveness of a society that to him was evident in a religious society. In this regard, then, it should be no surprise that Comte looked backward to the medieval period for example of the congruence of society and the institutions which defined it. The medieval world of course is not and cannot be our world today, filled as it was with a brooding sense of the presence of the supernatural. To this Comte is most opposed, for he is firmly committed to the view that the workings of nature are to be understood within the realm of scientific and not supernatural explanation.

Comte desired to provide something of a rudder for a society swirling with so many currents of thought and surmised a need to structure human society in conformity to scientific principles. He would construct, in effect, a science of society. From this idea, the discipline of sociology was born, for which Comte deserves the credit. Comte of course was not the first to attempt to laud nor attempt to capture the successes of the hard sciences in explaining phenomena of physics and chemistry and extend it to human subjects. Some previous Enlightenment figures had aspirations to do the same, but now Comte laid out a larger plan, complete with what might be called a philosophy of human history. In this history, Comte

contended that humankind had lived through three mental stages: the theological, the

metaphysical, and the positivistic. The stages reflect different and increasingly shifting

conceptualizations of the world. In the positivistic phase of human history, science comes into

its own, and the cumbersomeness of previous anthropocentric and metaphysical allusions of the

prior ages drop out. Man in a sense has the capacity to be happier because he no longer need

concern himself with things which in effect have no relevance to science. As they have no

relevance to science, they therefore have no relevance to human life. However, Comte's critics

sometimes charged that his plan for society involved lifting things from the museum of the

human past for use in the present. This charge was most lodged against Comte's sympathies for

a place for religious feeling within the realm of science, though not for God, but for Science.

If Comte had labored with creating a study of society with reference to scientific

principles, the net effect of Charles Darwin's theory of biological evolution was nothing less

than enormous upon thinkers, both in the sciences and the humanities. To a degree, it was

episodes like the Darwinian controversy that Comte's philosophy was designed to show the way

through, but in Comte's day, nothing quite as gigantic as a revolution in the life sciences had

happened quite yet. After the 1859 publication of his *The Origin of Species* by Darwin,

theologians as well as philosophers scrambled to reconfigure their thoughts on what to make of

"man." Of course there were thinkers and clergy who took on the plausibility of Darwin's theory,

though rarely with Darwin the man, but mostly with the pages of his book, and the renowned

debater, known as "Darwin's Bulldog," Thomas Huxley. Indicative of the ramifications of

Darwin's theory, it was Huxley himself who coined the term "agnostic" to indicate his position

on the age-old question of the existence of deity. Parties to the debate over Darwin's theory in great part are responsible for the cultural upheaval known as the great "Victorian Crisis of Faith." It seemed that what Darwin deemed man to be scientifically would have ramifications vastly beyond the scientific community. The philosophers, but also anthropologists, essayists, and novelists, to name but a few, would now take up a new conception of the human and the world in which he lived.

In time a cultural rift would become evident among intellectuals, though not the one we might think. That is, it would take about another century before observers started to take notice of the fact that two cultures of knowledge within Western intellectual culture were antagonists in their minimization of the other. In a famous lecture of 1959, C. P. Snow (1905– 1980) saw the cultural tear beginning with the Scientific Revolution. What eventually happened, and is quite evident to most still today, is what Snow called a "gulf of mutual incomprehension" between scientists and literary intellectuals, or as the latter are often described, those in the humanities. A university student of today, looking hard enough, can tell the difference between the two usually after only a minimal amount of time.

Huxley is as good a man as any to consider some of the fallout of Darwin's view of how the human species came into being. Darwin tried to steer clear of theological matters and the ultimate origin of man, but for more daring minds the writing was on the wall. Huxley spotted one conundrum. That is, if nature works in the way Darwin described, and nature in time produces the human species, how does one account for the fact, believed to be so by Huxley, that amoral nature produced a moral creature in the human species? Such an observation of course did not refute or overturn evolutionary theory (nor did Huxley have such intention), any more than the presence of evil in the world overturned the theist's belief in God. Huxley referred to the issue as humans having "kicked down the ladder by which we have come up." That is, just as soon as Darwin's theory had placed us solidly in the grip of nature, a consideration of human nature shows an offspring unlike its parent. Nevertheless, Huxley, like Darwin himself, kept his faith, that is, his agnosticism.

If belief in God survived Darwin the question then became where to locate God within this biological theory. For a time, and still today, one finds a sector of people affirming both. This has been difficult, however, because though nature may evidence a plan (unconscious of course), its workings are without mercy and grace, which previously flowed from the beneficent Christian God. Indeed, truth be told, nature is ruthless in its work. Of course nature was ruthless before Darwin's theory, but now a new lens is casting the concept of nature so as to highlight a mechanism that sends species out in the world in a struggle to the death. If this is the hand of God in the work of nature, then Nature's God must be no better than Nature—or so some thought.

Others came up with a philosophy that in time will be called "Social Darwinism." This philosophy attempts to somewhat legitimize the workings of the human world as simply following a law of survival like the law of the jungle, but in the contexts of the human population. The human's station in life, with regard for example to being rich or poor, is a measure of how well or how unwisely they have negotiated their human environment. If such is deemed a heartless philosophy, this is because it is, but it is faulted as such, returning to Huxley, because we have a revulsion toward the beastly manner in which nature operates. No one, save for the unrepentant Social Darwinist, could deem it "right."

In biology, the discipline out of which Darwin's theory arises, the human is now increasingly seen, not as made in any "image of God," but instead stamped with the characteristics of its primate ancestors. The human will therefore be seen in closer relationship with the natural mechanisms and laws which produced the species, and further from the Deity mistakenly counted the Creator in prior ages. The outcome in the war between science and religion seemed predictable with such narratives, despite the conundrums pointed up by the likes of Huxley. Indicative of the mounting secular forces of the nineteenth century, Karl Marx, on hearing of Darwin's work, was affirming of this latest blow to any notion of teleology remaining in science.

The philosophy of Herbert Spencer (1820– 1903) might seem the natural successor of Comte, with Darwin historically situated between them. Spencer, however, tends to look at the world, to include the human world from the perspective of the cosmos, almost as the Pre-Socratic philosopher might. Moreover, what dominates Spencer's thought within the cosmos is biological science, for obvious reasons. His metaphysic is constructed out of and from his understanding of that science. Spencer is perhaps, next to Hegel, the largest thinker of his age in that he attempts to amalgamate all knowledge to the point of some synthesis. However, he is more a cosmologist than a metaphysician, whereas Hegel is the reverse. Spencer, moreover, was particularly interested in man's metaphysical place in the larger cosmos; in this manner, for all of his allegiance to science, Spencer is an affirming humanist, as he sees grandeur in the human species and not simply humbling exercises for hopeful survival. He is interested in what we can infer about "man" from the new biological understanding of the world and life. This necessarily draws him into considering the human cosmically and this necessarily requires of him some comment on God or any being behind the cosmos.

However, Spencer resists thinking of God as object or an object, and more particularly, Spencer would not be congenial to much discussion of God at all. This is because he regards this conceptual entity as belonging to the mystery of Being, rather than the conclusion to any argument conceding or denying the existence of such a Being. In his philosophy, and in light of the influence of Darwin's theory, the previous idea of Deity is updated to "The Unknowable." Spencer, however, is hardly a pushy secularist in his desire to uphold a sense of the ultimate he finds in nature, but also in the heart of the human. At the same time, he maintains something of a scientific stance on such matters. Spencer, for example, like Darwin himself, took some account of Thomas Malthus's predictions of pressure on human population numbers. In Spencer's account, moreover, progress is at least partially prodded in awareness of this frightful pressure. Though very few read Spencer today, his ideas are worth noting, as streams of them are still touted as one way to deal with the chasm between religion and science.

Chapter 8
Twentieth-Century Philosophy

8. A. Critics of Hegel and the Rise of Analytic Philosophy

So lastingly influential was Hegel's philosophical system that virtually every major philosopher of the early twentieth century started out as a Hegelian. This includes Bertrand Russell and G. E. Moore and John Dewey, among others. Hegel worked on the big problems of philosophy and in the tradition of speculative philosophy, he is the last great metaphysician of Western philosophy. In the twentieth century no philosopher doing metaphysics rose to Hegel's stature, though some, like A. N. Whitehead, continued to do metaphysics, though not in a Hegelian mode, nor with nearly as many followers as Hegelian philosophy once counted. Compared to Hegel, Whitehead desired to save philosophy from the too zealous logical positivists of his era, while Hegel's efforts are partly cast toward saving philosophy from something of a crass materialism. The idealistic philosophy that Hegel came up with to do this, however, in time started to draw severe critics who scarcely ever relented in their mocking of a philosophy that held immense sway over much of Europe for close to a century.

Critics of Hegel at the end of the twentieth century, and in reaction against idealism, contended that philosophy should work on smaller and more manageable problems, and at the same time many of them often believed that metaphysical knowledge was impossible for philosophers anyway. (For this latter reason there was something of a "back to Kant" movement couched in rebellion against idealism and Hegel.) The beginning of rebellion against

Hegelianism, however, did not carry above it an insistence that metaphysics was impossible; philosophy did, however, need a good house cleaning, and generally the larger the philosophy or philosophical system, the more insistent the need for disciplined cleaning. In time, this general position and proclivity to engage more manageable issues in philosophy became known as analytic philosophy and tended to be a phenomenon of the English-speaking world. Today it is perhaps even more prominent among American philosophers than British thinkers, with an impressive philosophical influence almost as long-standing as that previously accorded Hegel.

European continental philosophers have been much less attracted to the analytic mode of doing philosophy for the most part. Continental thinkers have tended to be more historically minded, that is, setting the problems discussed in an historical framework, which necessarily enlarges the discussion. Analytic philosophers have tended to generally divorce the problem analyzed from historical context, sometimes so as to count such context irrelevant and impertinent to advancement in argumentation. Continental philosophy has also had something of a social temperament, blended with the historical canvas from which it works. That is, philosophy in this context is a means for social action or cultural transformation—the element of practice has a decided role in this mode of philosophy. Mention of some of the philosophies found within the continental tradition strongly exudes this connection: structuralism, psychoanalytic theory, hermeneutics, phenomenology, and, best known perhaps, Deconstructionism, Marxism, and Existentialism. Perhaps marking the greatest divide between philosophers in the analytic tradition from those of the continental tradition are differing judgments over the legacy of Hegel. That is, Continental thinkers to some degree are conscious heirs to the German philosopher. Analytic thinkers, by contrast, desired to leave Hegel in the dustbin of history.

The initial British criticism of Hegel was sparked by thinkers G.E. Moore (1873– 1958) and Bertrand Russell (1872– 1970), who began the twentieth century by rejecting the philosophy of Hegel which had permeated both Britain and America. Indicative of how powerful the Hegelian influence was, the previous and very strong empirical tradition in Britain, from Locke to John Stuart Mill, had retreated to the cellar in England during much of the nineteenth century under the predominance of Hegel in English universities. In time, however, British critics started to pick away at Hegel's philosophy. In many ways the rising British objection to Hegel was one of impatient common sense, and so not without reason the philosophy critics of Hegel advocated what was sometimes referred to as "common sense realism." They were not pragmatists, however, with Russell being notorious for his criticism of this American philosophy that he mocked almost as relentlessly as he did Hegel. In the first decade of the twentieth century, Russell and the pragmatist William James clashed on several occasions over their differing philosophies. Russell did not want truth subjugated to what he deemed a wrong theory (Hegel) or a wrong practice (James).

With Russell's later and particular attempt to align philosophy with science, but not to do the work of science, he was opting to work at clarifying our description of the world and reality. Like Moore, he was not averse to the attempt at metaphysics, but the muddled language of past metaphysics must be cleaned up with a rigor and a method Russell deemed largely absent in the history of philosophy. In time in Britain, Russell and other thinkers regained the historic British empirical leanings that the British have been noted for, and so the Hegelian metaphysic was abandoned. Moreover, as a mathematician and a philosopher, Russell manifested interest in the interface between logic and language. In this particular subject Russell found a worthy workmate for a time in his Austrian student, Ludwig Wittgenstein (1889– 1951), who, in 1919, published his monumental work, *Tractatus Logico-Philosophicus*.

Russell, however, was eventually not the only admirer of his student Wittgenstein, for upon publication of his book, a group of thinkers centered in Vienna, Austria and called the Vienna Circle and sometimes the logical positivists, started to take notice of Wittgenstein. These thinkers, unlike Moore and Russell, had as a central plank of their reason to be, the elimination of metaphysics from philosophy, as a matter of philosophical principle. The method of Wittgenstein in his book was of huge interest to them and in the 1920s the two sometimes met to discuss such matters. However, there were simply too many investors among members of the Vienna Circle in this largely unchartered way of doing philosophy for all to agree on how to proceed. Eventually volleys were launched between and among them and a kind of factionalism overtook the initial excitement of putting philosophy in its proper place and hat meant for the positivists, in the service of science. That much, for the time being, Russell could agree with the positivists.

Naturally enough this kind of discussion was highly technical, with the subject matter scarcely comprehensible to those outside of philosophy. For others, like Russell, there were other factors on the horizon drawing his attention. He, for one, could not proceed in ivory tower indifference to the coming conflict of World War I. Furthermore, in the decade of 1930, with the rise of Nazism and Adolph Hitler, many German and Central European thinkers migrated to North America, particularly the United States, to include the scientist Albert Einstein, the logical positivist Rudolph Carnap, and the theologian Paul Tillich. However, the effect of the two world wars on philosophy was varied. Philosophers of Jewish ethnicity, like Karl Popper and Edmund Husserl, were obviously affected by the anti-Semitism of the Nazi regime. By contrast, the philosopher Martin Heidegger has suffered in his subsequent reputation for his sympathies with Nazism during this period. Sartre's work in the French Resistance during the German occupation gave large impetus to his later literary and philosophical works. Russell himself, due to the unsafe conditions in the Atlantic during World War II, found himself for a while unable to return to his native Britain after a stay in America.

After World War II, analytic philosophy began to take a decidedly different turn from its beginnings with Russell and Moore. However, the initial scrutiny given to language, both by Moore and Russell in their different ways, did not dissipate but did change course. Russell had believed that because our ordinary way of speaking is muddled, clarification was required by transposing propositions into the formal and tighter language of logical symbolism. Other philosophers, however, would begin to demur. The attempt by Russell and others to root out vagueness and ambiguity by the aid of logic policing language, now met opposition in the analysis of ordinary language by others who wanted to uncover the meaning intended in ordinary language use. Moreover, after 1945, many in the analytic tradition turned their attention precisely to the analysis of ordinary language, to which Russell vehemently objected. Furthermore, Russell's formerly prized student Wittgenstein and his evoking of his famous discussion of "language games" produced a virulent critic in Russell. Not only was most of Russell's prior commitment to the logical ordering of language still intact and opposed to the new turn to "ordinary language" philosophy, Russell was most critical of what he regarded as the grave betrayal of philosophy. That is, for Russell this new form of philosophy stood prepared to let the world stand as it was—that is, in this conception, the job of philosophy was to understand, not to critique, the way people communicated. For Russell this was to divest philosophy of its birthright.

Meanwhile, in the previous decades the logical positivists had seemed to deny philosophy access to many of its traditional problems. Philosophy, therefore, looked like it was cornered and the question was, would there be any way out? With this kind of pressure, the heirs of the analytic movement in philosophy for the most part went their own individual way from the 1970s until the present. Therefore, characterizing these decades is almost as difficult as having to characterize the variegations of Renaissance philosophy. Nonetheless, some of the turns taken by self-acknowledged analytic philosophers evidence the attention to prohibited or at least suspect problems of the earlier generations of analytic thinkers. In other words, analytic philosophy has not proceeded the same way nor with the same set of problems throughout its history. The most noticeable is perhaps metaphysics, even though the subject is not tackled in the grandiose manner of the great metaphysicians of the past. The presumptive and dismissive attitude of most earlier analytic philosophers toward the history of philosophy has been diluted by the fact that within the analytic tradition of philosophy have arisen some able philosopher-historians of the movement. The previous dismissal of traditional philosophy as we find it most strongly in the logical positivists, to some degree, resembles the attitude of Descartes and Bacon toward their predecessors. Each has attempted to put philosophy in proper order by articulating a proper procedure to follow.

8. B. *The Logical Positivists and Science*

The logical positivists were in the ascendency in the early twentieth century and created a great stir in the philosophical world, in particular with their doctrine of verification. This group drew substantial attention because what they tried to accomplish in philosophy many had had hopes of doing, and if it could be done, so much the better for philosophy. The basic question was whether philosophy could somehow be interfaced or collated with science or scientific method, such that philosophy, previously and historically paltry in its findings and results, could manage analogous gains in knowledge so overwhelmingly evident in science. In the anxious attempt to do this, the positivists were animated with an optimistic enthusiasm nearly equal to that of the philosophers of the Enlightenment.

Characteristic of the positivists was a very critical attitude toward philosophy's previous penchant for unbridled, or at least unrewarded, speculation. This criticism meant that for the positivists the questions of philosophy would have to be reined in so as to have any possibility of finding answers. This would mean that philosophy should be permitted to address only those questions which, at least in theory, were answerable at the hands of science and scientific method. The questions that were so unfortunate so as to fall outside these parameters were summarily dismissed as "pseudo-questions" and regarded as meaningless. Therefore, the positivists were not so much separating truth from falsity, but signaling that any question or alleged answer to a question that could not be adjudicated as true or false was culpable of being tagged as meaningless. This criterion, famously referred to as the verification principle, mercilessly felled the questions of metaphysics and in time also removed ethics as a field of study for philosophy simply because ethical prescriptions could not be objectively vindicated. In effect the new program for philosophy was couched in the belief that only science has methodologies in place to decide or render a verdict to its questions. This is in contrast to the questions of theology and of course metaphysics which violate the rules for proper questions. The parameters of knowledge are the parameters of science. What proved most difficult for the group, however, was the attempt to demarcate in convincing detail that all pieces of scientific explanation could be tied, either directly or indirectly, to sensory adjudication. The logical positivists were therefore empiricists in epistemology, while the philosophy and epistemology of David Hume was hugely influential on this group.

The general idea of the positivists was that philosophy not science should be permitted to express beliefs or offer hypotheses that outran sensory perception. This idea necessarily placed them in the tradition of the radical empiricism of Hume, for Hume had tried valiantly to justify all of our knowledge as derivative from sense experience. The positivists would accordingly try to jettison all theoretical entities referred to in scientific explanation that lacked empirical ties. This attempt was simply an effort to abide by Hume's strenuous attempt at holding to empiricist strictures. Hume, however, forced the unmerciful examination of scientific terms (the example being his scrutiny of causality), but failed to find the concept derived from the reach of the human senses.

However energetic the positivist intention, their notion of proper science was that one must be ever vigilant to permit no stranger, or term, such as "force," to populate our scientific vocabulary without inspecting its sense data credentials at the door. This philosophical rite-of-passage would prove to be an impossible task, and equally, if not more difficult was to counter the charge from opponents that the verification principle was itself not verifiable. This means simply that if we are to assess the questions of the many fields of philosophy by the standard of a verification theory of meaning, to what precisely do we owe our obedience? That is, can the verification theory of meaning in effect meet the same standard of judgment whereby it presumes to judge? The final answer to this question after much haranguing among positivists and nonpositivist critics was no.

Though this school of thinking originated in a group of thinkers known as the Vienna Circle, it was not long in spreading its influence beyond members of the circle. The influence of the group was understandably strongest where empiricism had eminence, and so England

provided welcoming reception to a philosophical movement that acknowledged strong allegiance

to that doctrine. In addition, the travails in wartime Europe in the 1930s and 1940s sent many

able positivists, such as Rudolph Carnap, to American universities, where the doctrines of

positivism spread across the Atlantic. One of the ablest defenders of positivism in England was

A. J. Ayer, whose concise little book, *Language, Truth and Logic*, published in 1936, proved to

be a canonical text for positivists. However, indicative of the inability to make for consistency

in the positivist position, Ayer came out with a second edition ten years later, in which the

verification principle evidenced loss of some of its original luster, due to needed qualifications

compromising the earlier aura surrounding its reception.

The positivists at Vienna initially perceived they might have one of their ablest allies, not

in a member of the group—as able as they were—but in Russell's student Wittgenstein. The

group had fastened onto Wittgenstein's *Tractatus*, which in flavor and philosophical doctrine

appealed to the members of the circle. In that work the author, in reciprocating influences

between him and Russell, had attempted to bring or force language into a logical setting,

whereby the resulting analysis permits one to work between language and the logic it reveals.

By the end of this work, a certain exuberance was on view—and this point commendable to the

positivists when Wittgenstein wrote that if his conception of philosophy were correct, he had

solved all philosophical problems. This was entirely within the keeping of the positivist's

program, or so they thought. However, at conflict with this idea was the last sentence of the

Tractatus, where the author wrote that "Whereof one cannot speak, thereof one must be silent."

This sounded like the voice of a mystic speaking in the words of Wittgenstein, and in time this

perception of what Wittgenstein was up to put him out of favor with the group. Before such realization, however, the positivists were ecstatic, for a statement such as this seemed to them indicative of their own no-nonsense approach to truth claims with a willingness to exclude as "meaningless" whole chunks of human thought as lacking the necessary elements for adjudication. However, Wittgenstein was saying something very different. He appears to mean (there is still significant debate over the meaning of elements of Wittgenstein's philosophy) that the subjective element which is very strong in things like poetry, religion, and ethics excludes them from the domain of the philosopher. As such, then, philosophy is constrained by its inability to enter such sacred portals. Implied in this conception is not that poetry, religion, and ethics suffer, but in some way, that philosophy does. It is therefore understandable why it took the positivists some time before Wittgenstein's meaning in such statement took hold of them. He who had been welcomed in their ranks initially is in the end showed his way to the door.

Meanwhile, some years later Wittgenstein would go on to produce his own philosophy without them, and it would also be a philosophy uncongenial to Russell, his former teacher. Indeed, Russell would look on Wittgenstein's later philosophy as hardly worthy of the name. At the same time Russell and others easily discerned in Wittgenstein a personality who did not follow the ordinary human contours in his life. Never an ordinary academic by any stretch of the imagination, after his *Tractatus* was published in 1919 (some of it written while an Austrian soldier in World War I) he left Cambridge for a stint in Norway as a school teacher. Nevertheless, though away from philosophy and philosophers, this was apparently the time in which he initially began to develop a wholly different philosophy concerning language than that found in his *Tractatus*. Though this new philosophy was not published or put into a book until after his death as *Philosophical Investigations*, his ideas were influential through his teaching and oftentimes classroom notes were circulated among interested parties. Wittgenstein is thusan

154

example of a philosopher who wrote very little and nevertheless exercised formidable influence on Western philosophy. At the same time, his meaning is not always clear. His two published books are pregnant with almost Nietzschean aphorisms that students have endlessly debated.

In the radically different turn Wittgenstein makes in his second work, compared to the earlier *Tractatus*, he appears to prescribe nothing like a governing model to reveal the structure of the world, a task that had absorbed him in the earlier work. Rather, as he famously says, philosophers who take an opposite view have been "bewitched" by language in being blind to how language is actually used, as opposed to trying to make language an associate of the metaphysical task. In a word, Wittgenstein turns philosophy from prescription to description and as he famously writes, "philosophy leaves everything as it is." Philosophy, therefore, in his estimation, has gone off course, looking for something that can indeed be found, but is found in variegated and infinite forms in the multiplicity of ways we use the forms of language.

As radical as this "new" direction in philosophy may seem, it had antecedents even in Wittgenstein's day. When G.E. Moore was tutor to Wittgenstein, Wittgenstein would have heard Moore's habitual and famously intonated question, "what do you really mean?" on cross examination of an assertion. Wittgenstein accordingly became concerned to understand what people mean when they say something. The point, therefore, is not to correct language use, but to watch its varied workings. For Wittgenstein, always the particularist, the philosopher had too often judged language from the perspective of someone judging an engine when it is idling, rather than when the drive train is engaged and turning the wheels of the vehicle and taking the driver somewhere. In this sense, Wittgenstein's later philosophy is a philosophy of the living, not of immobile or certain logic.

8. C. The School of American Pragmatism

In turning to philosophy in America, one requires reminder that this nation is young compared to European nations and very young compared to much older Asian cultures. Even in its historical growth, there remains a retained vigor in the nation and people that still evokes the youthfulness and vigor of the nation. By contrast such a culture has also placed Americans at some remove from the contemplative spirit that traditionally characterizes philosophy and philosophers in older cultures. The visiting Frenchman, Alexis de Tocqueville, wrote in 1840 that "I think that in no country in the civilized world is less attention paid to philosophy than in the United States." America, it might be said, was a nation of movers and shakers and not precisely thinkers. To this day, historians and other students of the American nation continue to talk about an actual anti-intellectual spirit that resides in the culture at large. A second facet of American culture aligned with the aspect of youthfulness is that the culture is significantly, not to say predominately, driven by young people. This is in marked contrast to older European nations and in considerable contrast to Asian cultures, where age bolsters influence. Such factors and differences with other cultures do contribute to a certain dynamism certainly witnessed in most often the larger cities in America.

With such youthfulness on display, it might seem that philosophy could hardly make inroads, save for the relatively assured enclave of universities. However, the religious heritage of America provided for some philosophical thinking, with Jonathan Edwards (1703– 1758) of New England counted usually as the first significant thinker of the then English colony. Though more a theologian than a philosopher per se he was hugely drawn to Locke's philosophy. Edwards took significant interest also in Isaac Newton's scientific work, which during Edward's lifetime was pushing thinkers in Europe and some in America to veer toward deism, though not Edwards. In trying to place a figure like Edwards into the broader history of Western philosophy, he is seen as perhaps the last of the medieval Scholastic philosopher-theologians or perhaps as the first in a string of American philosopher-theologians. This debate and the subtleties of Edwards's thought, however, are usually lost on those who only know Edwards for his 1741 sermon, "Sinners in the Hands of an Angry God."

The significant founders of the American nation from the British Colony in North America made extensive use of John Locke's writings, but whereas Edward's interest lay in Locke's empiricism, it was Locke's political philosophy that they, led by Thomas Jefferson (1743– 1826), made appeal. Though at significant odds with the British government at the time, the strong tradition of parliamentary rule and English individualism and something of a bootstrap insistence on independence found ready acceptance from colonists now prepared to make their own nation from largely British ideals. The Declaration of Independence, largely written by Jefferson, was first and foremost inspired by Locke's ideas.

The first six American presidents brought immense learning and erudition to their office and also largely, though not exclusively, a deist orientation in religion. Some self-identified with the European Enlightenment, like Jefferson and Thomas Paine (1737– 1809). Eventually, primarily under the guidance of Jefferson, attempt was made to keep the institutions of religion and political governance distinct. (Paine eventually fell out of favor for being too antireligious.) A religious freedom which had often been absent in Europe was desired by many of the American immigrants who undertook their voyages to this new place for precisely such reason. Prominent among these were some Puritans from East Anglia in England, who began to make their home in New England in the New World in the 1630s.

Nevertheless, the early architects of American culture wanted to make the colony and then their nation with some institutions modeled from Europe. From this desire grew the great universities, beginning with Harvard College in 1636, initially populated by faculty of overtly Puritan leanings. This institution and others are still with us today, though with different intellectual predilections than their predecessors. Edwards had gone to Yale University, instituted in 1701. The eventual Columbia University began classes in 1754 with a mere eight students, and one faculty member, Samuel Johnson, the first President of what was then called King's College. Princeton University was founded in 1746. Jefferson himself started the institution of William and Mary in Virginia. With the founding of Cornell University in Ithaca, New York, in 1865, a nonsectarian institution came into being.

Philosophies with some American distinctives began to take root by the middle of the nineteenth century, while others continued to reflect orientations European in origin. David Hume's philosophy, found too skeptical by fellow Scottish philosophers, had provoked the common-sense realism of Thomas Reid (1710– 1796), which had been accorded strong reception from Protestant communities in Scotland and those migrating to America. Reid's philosophy indeed appeared to be a philosophy for the common man, requiring no elaborate or exaggerated epistemological machinations. James McCosh (1811– 1894) took the lead in this philosophy at Belfast in Ireland and then as president of Princeton University, promulgating this thinking into great popularity. Other thinkers in this tradition veered toward German idealism with suspicions cast toward the belief in materialism that was gaining adherents along with positivism. The stronghold for idealism, however, came with a group in the mid-west of America, self-styled the St. Louis Hegelians. Brandishing some affiliations with New England Transcendentalists, this group focused on devising a philosophy which would give legitimacy to philosophy concerning religion. Some looked to the thought of the French philosopher Victor Cousin (1792– 1867) who, as these Americans were now doing, had to sort out intellectual options and directions to take for the future. This meant something on the order of articulating a philosophy commensurate with suitable religious beliefs.

As much as these inclinations were shared by and equally serious inquiries for European counterparts, perhaps nothing attracted European attention more than the thought of American Transcendentalism. Here two American notables gave considerable publicity to a variant current of thought highly reminiscent of the nearly contemporary movement of Romanticism in England. Drawing upon some Taoist influences, Ralph Waldo Emerson (1803– 1882) and Henry David Thoreau (1817– 1862) made an appeal to the religious element of nature in their philosophy. (Emerson was the godfather of later American philosopher, William James.) Thoreau of course is famous for his work *On Walden Pond* and no less so for his 1848 essay "On Civil Disobedience," which dovetails nicely with Emerson's emphasis on the individual.

Emerson, however, provoked significant uproar with a speech presented in 1838 at Harvard's School of Divinity. Unorthodox as his philosophical religion was to the orthodox, Emerson possessed something of the practical man's indifference to what quibbling philosophers contended, by himself scoffing at the scoffers. More like a religious seer than an obtuse philosopher perhaps, he had little temperament for systemization. For all his esoteric doctrines, however, Emerson did not place his thoughts within the debate between the materialist and the idealist. He did nonetheless place his thinking in the vicinity of idealism rather than materialism, but with too few specifics to satisfy philosophers closer to idealism than Emerson. For other critics, Emerson simply aligns the human too closely to nature and nature too closely to God. Therefore, the charge of pantheism was frequent against him.

Philosophy in America during the nineteenth century continued to reflect something of the American religious character, as manifested in the case of the Transcendentalists, but soon with thinkers willing to grapple with other challenges to religion. This was certainly the case with William James (1842– 1910), the great American pragmatist philosopher, who had first been a student of psychology. He was drawn to philosophy by precisely something akin to what some American thinkers were laboring under—the squeeze of science and the implied materialism often accompanying it with reference to human free will and religious belief. James lived in an age when some must have surely thought that religious belief would grow ever weaker against the competence and competition of science. However, James jumped into the fray to argue for the cogency and practical benefit of religious belief in a skeptical age. To a great degree, James's issue was close to that of Kant: that is, to reconcile a religious and moral view of the world with the view of science.

James had the psychologist's eye for the mind and world of religious people, starting with fervent religious persons. In his famous survey of religion in the world, entitled *The Varieties of Religious Experience*, he conceded that religious genius was often accompanied by a personality deemed almost mad on occasion. He made the comparison, moreover, that admired intellectuals in other fields were sometimes similar in peculiarities, but that in an age of natural suspicion toward religion, the religious genius was apt to be regarded as a crank. In his *Will to Believe*, James attempted to chart a way to religious belief exhibiting the practical benefits of beliefs working. As part of his pragmatic attempt to steer clear of metaphysical Hegelianism, he contended that one could still be a good empiricist in so doing and without taking flight to idealism.

John Dewey (1859– 1952), a second American pragmatist philosopher, was primarily a social philosopher who exercised much influence over formal education in American classrooms and classroom laboratories. His general theory of education is that students learn better and more by doing than by being told; he therefore stood opposed to memorization and formalized learning. Dewey had been a primary and high school teacher, whereas James had trained as an MD, but never practiced. Dewey was concerned with societal problems and issues he deemed fixable from pragmatic principles. His book *Reconstruction in Philosophy* evidences Dewey as impatient with a past which needed displacement for the sake of new directions. His democratic theory was one in which social institutions made for success. In this, Dewey shows something of a departure from the ordinary American notion of prizing individualism. Similarly indicative of his social thinking, Dewey was signatory to the Humanist Manifesto of 1933. Unlike James, he wrote a notable volume, *Art as Experience*, on aesthetics, where he tended to blur the distinction between the artist and the community from which the artist works. A close look at his religious views, particularly in his *A Common Faith*, reveals Dewey trying to position religion as functioning for the purpose of unifying society, and not, as it had often done in the past, he contended, serving to fracture society. Interestingly, Dewey, like so many others of his day, had started out as a Hegelian. Moreover, his influence in education has sometimes trumped his legacy in philosophy.

By the time of Dewey's death in 1952, the analytic tradition of philosophy from England had already migrated to America, and would soon dominate the American scene in philosophy. Of particular note are W.V.O. Quine (1908– 2000), who came from a stream of analytic philosophers intent to make philosophical method as respectable and as resourceful as scientific method. Quine, however, was deeply critical of the logical positivists. The American historian of science, Thomas Kuhn (1922– 1996), cast some doubts on the presumed safety of scientific reasoning to ensure objectivity, by indicating something of the subjective context of much presumed scientific decision making. The net effect was to make science look less than only scientific.

The appearance of other social philosophies other than pragmatism is also evident by mid-century in the school of Objectivism of the Russian-American Ayn Rand (1905– 1982), who, somewhat like some of the Existentialists, wrote her philosophy into her novels. However, and from a very different perspective on political philosophy, came John Rawl's (1921– 2002) tome, *A Theory of Justice*, which has had immense and continuing influence in this field of philosophy. Alasdair MacIntyre (b. 1929) remains perhaps the most eminent ethicist and political philosopher in a Thomist mold. Alvin Plantinga (b. 1932), a notable analytic philosopher of the Reformed Epistemology school, is probably the most famous living philosopher of religion. Pragmatism, moreover, has seen some recent resurgence in the work of Richard Rorty (1931– 2007), who self-identified himself as a postmodern philosopher from within the ranks of pragmatism. Thomas Nagel (b. 1937) has been prominent in philosophy of mind and ethics as well as political philosophy. His writings not infrequently brush up against religious topics.

8. D. *The Philosophy of Existentialism*

In the work of Edmund Husserl (1859– 1938), one encounters the effort to construct a study of human consciousness through a philosophy of phenomenology. Husserl significantly influenced both Martin Heidegger and John Paul Sartre, and thus Husserl must be counted as a significant contributor to the foundations of the twentieth-century philosophical movement of Existentialism.

Husserl sounded the existential theme when he wrote his *Philosophy and the Crisis of European Man*. His chief argument in this work was that philosophy and reason and rationality had increasingly lost their way in a modern age where the methods of the natural sciences pronounce upon all fields. What had started out in Greek philosophy as an attempt, such as we see in Socrates, to understand ourselves and the world through reason, descends in modernity to an insistence upon bringing to bear upon all subjects of study, with no exceptions, the methodologies of the natural sciences. The reductive method that follows should raise the question of the applicability of this method to subjects outside these sciences. Husserl raises the point because the realm of the nonphysical or spirit is subjected to an alien analysis when it is twisted in such fashion by the tools of the natural sciences. By contrast, Husserl wants to recover the world we experience: the world we live in is the world encountered in our experience. It is this world, not the world seen through the lens of the natural sciences, that Husserl wants to capture in his phenomenological approach.

Martin Heidegger (1889– 1976) had been a student of Husserl, though Heidegger's writings evidence some substantial disagreements with Husserl. It would be Heidegger and Sartre who would contribute the weightiest and most difficult tomes to enunciating the particulars of the philosophy of Existentialism. Heidegger's famous work, *Being and Time*, is perhaps the most esteemed classic in Existentialist philosophy. In this work, Heidegger is insistent that the human being cannot simply be counted as another being existing in a universe of beings. Furthermore, the human being is certainly not a thing. As such, he is not really an object, nor an object with properties, as he has so often been accounted by many philosophers. Rather, humans exist in a realm that is and is not theirs, called Being. As such they are aware that their state of Being is one whereby they can choose to interact with their station in certain ways. That is, the realm of Being in which they exist is one in which, as Sartre contended, they "show up." This produces some anxiousness, per awareness that their modality of existence possesses a certain precariousness, highlighted on the other end of life by the looming fact that their being in the world is limited, that is to say, finite.

The human, armed with this kind of awareness of his mode of being, and unlike objects or other things in the world, considers himself in his uniqueness. That is, he has the capacity to ruminate over himself and to realize that he has responsibility for himself. In other words, he makes himself by his decisions. He is aspiring or not aspiring to be, and so "authenticity" becomes important in Heidegger and Sartre, as well as other philosophers of Existentialism. Suffice it to say that a whole literature has come into existence that reflects the themes relatively common to that philosophy known as Existentialism. Of course Sartre himself contributed to that literature, perhaps most famously with his *Nausea*. Albert Camus (1913– 1960), though an existential philosopher in his own right, chiefly as revealed in his popular *The Myth of Sisyphus and Other Essays*, is nonetheless better known from his fictional works reflecting existentialist themes. Such works would be *The Plague* and *The Stranger*. Perhaps one body of fictional work most associated with existential themes is the work of the Czech writer Franz Kafka (1883– 1924), particularly *The Trial*. In this book a man is arrested and finally executed. In the agonizing time between the two events he makes a valiant but vain attempt to discover what the charge against him is.

As indicated, Existentialism tended to focus upon the individual, expressing suspiciousness toward an objectivity appearing to swallow up or ignore the particularities of individuals. This necessarily put existentialists in opposition to much previous philosophy. The existentialists of the twentieth century, furthermore, could count among their number such predecessors as Pascal, Kierkegaard, and Nietzsche. Existentialism proved to be a philosophy that had much appeal to people hardly acquainted with traditional or academic philosophy. However, despite its numerous critics, Existentialism proved to be more than a simple cultural fad or even more than a philosophical fad in Western philosophy. However, some of its thinkers, particularly Heidegger and Sartre, even on a dedicated and protracted study of their works, may prove as baffling as anything Hegel ever wrote. In this context Heidegger was frequently paraded by the logical positivists as a deserved whipping boy for his metaphysical excesses in the use of language and assertions. Existentialists, however, did not for the most part aspire to logical purity for the largely unacknowledged reason that the human—the subject of their work —was a more slippery subject that what logic allowed. Man may be the "measure of all things," as the good humanist Protagoras contended, but measuring the measurer proved the most difficult task of all.

The existentialists took on the subject of man after historical philosophers before them abandoned the subject, or, as Husserl complained, forced the human as a subject into the form of an object. In this enterprise of faulting one's predecessors, the existentialists were not the first by any means. That is, the history of philosophy by and large exhibits precisely the sort of criticism whereby the philosopher or thinker repudiates mistakes or countenances his predecessors. This he does by way of laying the groundwork for a new start on an old subject. We see this almost from the beginning of Greek philosophy, with Socrates, but more robustly in Aristotle who critiques his Pre-Socratic predecessors. Kant too criticized his rationalist and empiricist predecessors and opined that he had in effect created another Copernican Revolution, but this one in epistemology, not cosmology. Hegel, moreover, before he lays out his impressive system, stops to countenance why Kant's contended barriers to doing metaphysics could be brushed aside, with the metaphysical project resumed over Kant's faulty objections.

The existentialists, therefore, in a new take and directions on an old subject—the human—were not the first to criticize their predecessors. They were, however, while not completely novel in their approach, seemingly prepared to present the human in a light that somewhat followed from the prior thinking mixed in with Romantic criticisms of rationalism. The existentialists did not like frozen or fixed man, and neither did the Romantics. This is why not a few commentators on the existentialists refer to them (and sometimes the Romantics) collectively as irrationalists. However, given that the existentialists for the most part want to paint a neglected, that is to say, a whole picture of man, their picture is profoundly different. Nietzsche had to a degree prepared the way in his groundbreaking study of the Greeks. These Greeks had previously been portrayed as the pinnacle of rationalism, with nothing underneath but the steel of reason. Moreover, with Nietzsche's characterization of the Apollian and Dionysian Greek, the road was paved to fill out the mixed Greek personality beyond being defenders of reason and rationality. Furthermore, with Sigmund Freud's revelations about the nature of human nature in full light in the twentieth century with two world wars, Existentialism had plenty of source material from which to talk about and present humans in a new light.

Soren Kierkegaard (1813– 1855) had attended Hegel's lectures in Berlin, but grew to despise Hegel's philosophy as suffocating. Kierkegaard contended that Hegel's philosophy, concerned as it was with objectivity, lost sight of individual subjects, namely people. To Kierkegaard Hegel made the human person a simple cog in the machine, and Kierkegaard reacted by exalting the human subject over any object. Kierkegaard's philosophy was not a philosophy of "me-ism" however, but a philosophy which accentuated the extraordinary requirements of personhood. Kierkegaard, for example, laid great stress upon commitment, participation, consciousness, decision, and action, and impugned the notion of the human as an idle spectator in a world in which things simply happen to them. Furthermore, Kierkegaard tends to undermine the solidity and depreciate the value of objectivity as a notion separating the individual subject from truth. Kierkegaard therefore offered the notion of "Truth is subjectivity." Kierkegaard does not mean by such a concept that the individual can create their own truth, but he does mean that a truth that I have not made my own is not really a truth for me. This may sound rather like Kant's ethical notion that one's morality should be genuinely one's own and not borrowed from elsewhere, which would make it ultimately foreign to the user. Thus our morality should be in Kant's terms "self-legislated." In so doing, placing ourselves in charge of ourselves—a point of Enlightenment thinking—resembles a theme of the existentialists.

Jean-Paul Sartre (1905–1980) is probably the best known existential thinker in the twentieth century. However literary Sartre was, and he is that, he was also capable of producing a great philosophical treatise, namely his *Being and Nothingness*. The revolt against Hegel took many forms, but a glance at Sartre's voluminous work reveals that he is lacking in neither metaphysical astuteness nor pungent phrase. Sartre, in some ways like the Germans Karl Jaspers, but particularly Martin Heidegger, was intent on burrowing down into the existentialist topic— "Being," and making sense of the human predicament in such a manner. Existentialism was not, therefore, with some lesser exceptions, a group of avant-guarde artists trying to climb up the philosophical ladder with a pretense of being something they were not.

Sartre illustrates in another way, too, the great variety among existentialists, for he was an atheist while Kierkegaard was an overt Christian thinker who deemed many cultural features of his day (to include the Danish State Church) as so many avoidances of God. This difference pertains more to the human focus that is their subject of inquiry, and necessarily draws into the discussion the question of man's being in relation to other possible things, such as "Being." The notable existentialists are almost to a man humanists in a way that Hegel and the metaphysical architects of his following were almost oppositely scholastics and tied to a method that Kierkegaard would contend, bound and gagged them.

The themes among dissimilar existentialists, therefore, tend to be similar. Among the many features of Sartre's philosophy few stand out so prominently as his emphasis upon human freedom. Sartre is famous for his statement that "existence precedes essence." He meant by this that we decide what we are and what we will become, and that it is us who does this. There is no prefabricated definition of a human to which we humans shall strive to emulate. Thus the "essentialism" of Plato is out. To adopt essentialism, according to Sartre, would be to abdicate the responsibility of being human, for the essence of humanity is not deduced from *a priori* definition, but is the result of actual living choices made as we act out our lives. In effect we make ourselves up (define ourselves) as we go along. This should not be thought to suggest that we can be irresponsible, for indeed, all the grave responsibility of what we are is up to us. Thus, rather than lessening human responsibility, it is heightened and weighted in Sartre's conception. This is the meaning of Sartre's equally important statement, that man is "condemned to be free."

However much aspects of Existentialism are akin to the prior Romanticism, Sartre's meaning is far from Rousseau's contention that man is born free, but that he is everywhere in chains. In other words, Rousseau faults society for taking a human and bending him into a form that is alienating to him. Rousseau, in short, is willing to cast blame and dispersions around the individual, without faulting the individual first and foremost. Sartre does not indulge the individual, but holds him and not the things around him accountable for what the individual becomes. This is why Sartre is adamant to dismiss even the slightest suggestion that the human

is determined by laws denying human freedom.

Chapter 9
Postmodern Philosophy

9. A. Antecedents of Postmodern Thinking

Both Romanticism and Existentialism prefigured elements of what is called today postmodern thinking. If modern philosophy was characterized by a close and disciplined association with science, beginning with Descartes and Bacon and continuing into the twentieth century with the efforts of logical positivists, postmodern philosophy is characterized by criticism of the marks of objectivity held up as the hallmark of scientific thinking. Indeed, the preferences and directions of postmodern thinking may appear to indicate the virtual abandonment of traditional philosophy, as when Nietzsche, for example, writes that he prefers Homer to Plato. Western thinkers hitherto had assumed there was progress in the progression of thinking from Greek mythology to Greek rationalism and beyond. Postmodernity, however, largely contends against such presumptions.

The rationalism of modern thinking is under intense scrutiny from the perspective of postmodernism, often making postmodernism appear to critics as dedicated to irrationalism. Undeniably, a strong affirmation of relativism in postmodernity seems evident, reminiscent of the Sophists who Socrates battled with over this very issue. In an affirmation of this relativism, Nietzsche goes so far as to contend that "truth is a kind of error," or, as Richard Rorty, the postmodern philosopher offers, truth is "what your colleagues will let you get by with saying." With such contentions it seems that philosophy, as the attempt to get to the bottom of things as the goal of rational thought, is impugned. Prior historical efforts to dig to the foundations is

171

abandoned, with the ravenous epistemological appetites of modernity now deemed spurious. The disrespect accorded variant voices and opinions of the past is deemed in a postmodern ethos intolerable.

To the modern rationalist defending his position the postmodern turn looks like an infuriated popular culture in rebellion against the cultural or intellectual riches of an age scarcely understood. Stronger said, to the unrepentant and reasoning modernist, there may seem little more than envy of modernism in postmodern critique of modernism. Paradoxically such a critique of postmodernism is not dissimilar to the critique of the postmodernist that the fights over knowledge and similar scuffles of the past were little more than power struggles. To the postmodernist, these scuffles were very far from the deceitful claim of self-proclaiming elites to pursing truth; instead they were indicative of a raw pursuit of power, masquerading as something more prestigious. This is why the field of the sociology of knowledge quickly became a reinvigorated field of study around mid-twentieth century. Suddenly, great interest surrounded the question of how the goals, aims, and answers of modern thought came to be. Among other questions, queries were raised like "who owns knowledge?" with the implication that, somewhat similar to Rorty, that ownership of what qualified as knowledge gave immense power to those relegating to themselves the authority of making such a claim and closing the gate behind themselves. With book titles like *The Social Construction of Reality*, the thesis suggested was that truth might be an underhanded plaything, such that those who claimed to own it could thereby exercise power over those presumed lacking it. Within such a consideration, the work of the French philosopher Michel Foucault found fertile ground. With Foucault the Olympian conception of knowledge would be scrutinized from the ground level in his 1961 work, *Madness and Civilization*. Augmenting this kind of investigation, the historian of science Thomas Kuhn, though denying any absolute undermining of scientific objectivity in his very influential *The Structure of Scientific Revolutions*, seemed to others to do just that. This new story of the history of actual science being carried out was close enough to the new thinking to more than jolt the many disciplines it affected.

A revolutionary spirit was now afoot in much of philosophy and disciplines within the humanities. Some of this spirit was captured in a new field of studies referred to as Cultural Studies. The philosophy within this discipline, however, is not confined to its own borders, but stretches out in influence to touch other disciplines. Cultural Studies purports to scrutinize political motivations that dominate cultures and that dictate much of the lives of what might be called innocent people. A recent example is the contention that within a culture there are "privileged" positions or voices which drown out or subvert or deny voice to other promising but deprived aspirants. Not a few critics have contended that the motifs of the discipline are dominated by political agendas that subvert the discipline to serve political purpose. That is, with literature or philosophy, as examples, ideologies serve to dominant study, and thus the discipline manifests more political allegiance than allegiance to the discipline per se. The discipline is thus the plaything of the governing ideology. One might contend that the charges and counter-charges leveled in this debate paradoxically reveal that both disputants concede that some underhandedness is at work in how their disciplines work—or do not work. In other words, the old Olympian notion of objectivity separated from any bias is largely denied by both parties. Nevertheless, defense of Olympian objectivity, particularly in the hard sciences, still remains strong. However, postmodern critics will charge such defenders with the naiveté of supposing that human hands do not taint the projects we construct, whether consciously or unconsciously.

Such a debate of course is corollary to the debate over the perspective from which subject matter is presented or taught. As example, there has been no little debate in the last decades over the Western perspective of "eurocentrism," referring to the fact that much of the history of the West has been presented from the perspective of the West. Implied in the charge of eurocentrism is not only complaint against the narrow-mindedness of such perspective. Stronger complaint is lodged against the bias of a perspective essentially ignoring contributions of the tertiary cultures and nations which have been subjugated in the heroic but dubious journey of the West to dominance. Privilege was the outcome of this dominance. The history of the West therefore has been written by Western participants, or, as some historians are inclined to quip, "by the winners." The underlying criticism of bias is clear.

One way of compensating for omission and like injustices done to less privileged peoples, is to give them their previously denied voice. In this ambience, a basic education may come down to instilling in readers and learners not just the desire, but indeed the mandate to "change the world." The advancement and support of such an idea lie behind much of the sloganeering of many institutions of higher learning today. Allied with this impetus is the not infrequently observed guilt-ladenness of academics working in ivory tower cloisters who perceive the real and greater work of the world is that of bringing social justice for the world into reality. The inclination to bring the world of correct thinking to bear upon making a correct world may be suggested as the real purpose of education. Paradoxically, however much this puts the real work of the classroom outside the classroom, it is also indicative of how powerful a classroom can be. It can produce soldiers as ready to march as any of the past.

If much of such a culture is indication of significant departure from a modern epoch, to many critics it is more basically a reflection of a society which has lost nearly all directions for pursuance of truth. Nevertheless, however irrational postmodernism may seem to those dismayed by it, part of what is fundamentally at issue in the postmodernist debate is the propriety of the modern notion of "truth," and its modern measure, or at times near equivalent, rationality. Fear of what becomes of truth when the presumed solidity of objectivity and rationality are questioned provokes intense debate in the philosophy of science, and of course, the perennial obsession of modern Western thought—epistemology. In modernity it was science that seemed to provide the greatest haven for objectivity and immunity from irrationality and subjectivity. While the postmodern turn may be derided as the literary turn and as but another "escape from reason," this is because science and philosophy in modernity have for the most part excluded forms of discourse other than themselves on any question of truth.

The rationalist frenzy of modernity reached its peak in the "scientific philosophy" of a group of thinkers, the logical positivists, who convinced themselves they were empiricists when in reality they were apriorists. To the positivists the only sure truths were truths unaffected or unamenable by anything human, while their disdain for nonobservable entities and theoretical constructs was prompted by fear of objective truth becoming less so by subjective input. These obsessions were so strong among positivists that they attempted to exchange the philosophical enterprise for the scientific one in the hope of insuring real truth and objectivity.

Standing in the historical transition between the premodern poetic and mythical traditions of ancient Greece and the birth of Western philosophy, Plato had to battle the power of the poets and the Greek mythical tradition for the rationalism and the rational god of philosophy. With postmodernism there is a reopening of the "ancient quarrel between poetry and philosophy" after over two millennia in which philosophy, reason, and finally science in their various forms sought the attenuation or expurgation of everything not themselves on the question of truth. In the conflict between the two, there is some resemblance of postmodernism to the Romantic

resistance to Enlightenment rationalism. The conflicts within philosophy are seldom *sui generis*.

In the heyday of positivism, any philosophy that veered away from the logical and

presumed scientific techniques of positivist philosophy was given the choice of calling itself

"poetry" or "nonsense." The positivist's judgment upon any discourse as "poetry" was for them

an assumption of the difference, and the distance, between scientific philosophy and other forms

of discourse. In postmodern thought, both this difference and distance is contested, and is even

being denied. With postmodernism there is the attempt to overcome a perceived pretentious

inherited rationalist tradition by posing it against other traditions of diverse discourse. To some,

it seems like a breath of fresh air. To others it seems like a train-wreck of Western civilization.

9. B. The End of Philosophy?

Bertrand Russell castigated his student Ludwig Wittgenstein as being partially

responsible for turning philosophy into a study of the silly ways in which silly people say silly

things, or, as the derided philosophy was sometimes more respectfully named, "Ordinary

Language Philosophy." Russell felt strongly that pursing this misdirection in philosophy was

tantamount to giving up philosophy. The business and work of philosophy was to ask the

penetrating questions that made for discovery and hopefully knowledge, Russell thought. This

enterprise was not for the faint of heart, though Russell was sensing by the 1940s that what

began as the analytic school of philosophy that he and his colleague G. E. Moore had spawned at

the turn of the century, would now often pursue philosophy differently than he and Moore.

Wittgenstein had famously written that philosophy leaves things as they are. To thinkers like

Russell, however, such a motif led philosophers to abandon the ship of discovery that the voyage of philosophy had undertaken for so long.

Perhaps fatigue in doing the hard work of philosophy had prompted a change of course, but one can also contend that philosophy had changed course multiple times during its long history in the West. In other words, tumult, and at times significant tumult, had been a feature of the history of philosophy. Certainly the eclipsing of the various Roman philosophies of late antiquity into medieval Christian scholastic philosophy is one such change of direction. Another occurs when Renaissance philosophy started to put renewed but also a different emphasis into subjects like the human world, compared to medieval conceptions. Furthermore, however much the thought of Descartes and Bacon still had strings attached to prior medieval philosophy, it is clear that with them and their resultant influence, that philosophy for the future would be revamped from its existing course.

Perhaps the greatest change in the direction of philosophy within the history of philosophy occurs in relationship to science. The distinction between the two disciplines in ancient thought was not and could not be finely demarcated at the time. By contrast, by the time of the early modern age, and particularly in the thought of Bacon, the difference between the two pushed some thinkers in the direction of an alliance, however hazy still, between science and the empirical method. The older but increasingly impugned philosophical and particularly Aristotelian apparatus that had accompanied the quest for knowledge was given notice. Though Aristotle himself was certainly more empirical in his philosophical leanings than his teacher Plato, Aristotle was deemed too tied to a conceptual world that made him and his followers beholden to speculation too remote from experimental verification. However, there was another fork in the road. An abiding distinction among early modern thinkers is fairly apparent in comparing the thoughts of Bacon to Descartes, where Bacon's inclination toward inductive methodologies is to be contrasted to Descartes's greater reliance upon mathematics and deduction. As remarked in our chapter on Early Modern Philosophy, for all the stellar discoveries that mathematical tools in part provided for the early scientists of modernity, it took more time to realize that knowledge of the world required one to be in the world, in a manner of speaking. One could not simply deduce the nature of the world from only thinking logically about the world, however impressive any such deductive systemization might appear.

Later, John Locke's empiricist epistemology contributed to an understanding of how derivative from our experience in the world was our conceptual machinery. However, in the next century Kant would argue against the empiricists that the categories or concepts within the human mind were required to frame an intelligible experience of the world, but did so as a reflection of the human mind rather than the world studied. In this scenario, we might say that the status of the world of scientific knowledge seemed beholden to something of an assumed idea from scientists—that is, that scientific knowledge of the world was something more than knowledge of how humans thought.

Nevertheless, scientists of then and now most often feel no obligation to bow before the verdicts of the philosophers. The desire of the philosopher to have or want more puts the philosopher not only at significant remove from the common man, but also oftentimes from scientific man. Science seems in the rightful hands of scientists; what, moreover, if anything, is or should be, in the hands of the philosopher, except to be perhaps a perpetual questioner? This is a pertinent question and especially so in an age dominated by the cultural prestige accorded science. For this and other reasons the scientist is rarely doubting for a minute that their conceptions of the world match to a great degree the structures of the world. Like the philosophical pragmatists, the scientist usually takes it as enough if his ventured theory or product survives exposure to reality via experiments and verifications.

In an age dominated by science, the philosopher nevertheless still has room to work, if he remains willing to do the kind of humanistic work first chartered out by Socrates, though frequently shoved aside in some philosophical and scientific quarters of today. The omission of the Socratic challenge in part has produced in the past some dissidents and dissident movements. In the modern past these have generally been Romanticism, Phenomenology, and Existentialism, and, to some degree, Ordinary Language Philosophy. More in the present, however, one could place postmodernism. The emphasis upon the human living in the world, and not just in the world of the philosopher, is discernable in not a few philosophers within the history of philosophy.

If epistemology in the modern world was captivated by the role of the intellect and the senses with reference to knowledge, another group of philosophers emerging in the nineteenth century—though with prior antecedents like Blaise Pascal—began to emphasize the role of the human will in explaining the world and the human. If prior philosophers for the most part had launched reason as their rudder into the world, this group drew attention to the way the human will can will the world or themselves to be. Arthur Schopenhauer was certainly a pioneer in this kind of philosophy, and given his topic of interest he became a student of the Hindu *Upanishads*. As a once avid reader of Schopenhauer's philosophy of Will, Frederick Nietzsche develops a whole philosophy of will with reference to culture, and like many of the later existentialists, will take up the story form as one way to enunciate his ideas.

For such thinkers, the world of the philosopher had grown too suffocating and narrow by its slavish following of reason. Some of them sought to restore the element of the human back to a philosophy that had careened out of orbit, strenuously objecting to something like the

179

contemporary Thomas Nagel's touted "view from nowhere." The objection would be that every person, after all, lived somewhere, and none lived "nowhere." In Nagel's perspective, the view from nowhere was the idealized state of perspective, and where science wanted to be so as to ensure objectivity. Little wonder, then, that thinkers like Kierkegaard preferred subjectivity. The objectors, as in Kierkegaard, wanted to rescue the human from the excessively rational element of philosophy where the human had been lost or, perhaps more accurately described, confined.

Part of the reason for debate about the end or future of philosophy is that there is long-lasting debate over what is the proper subject or purpose of philosophy. Added to this is the fact that as philosophy appears to own no particular subject matter, except what we might describe as the unknown—on which philosophy in general hopes to shed some light—philosophy may look like something rather extraneous to the real advance of knowledge. This seems more or less much of the criticism of Bacon toward philosophy. Further forward in the modern period, moreover, we find the logical positivists most adamant to force philosophy into a framework or methodology, where, like science, it can produce some confident results because there are established procedures.

This move in itself is reflective of the fact that oftentimes, and particularly in the modern period, philosophers have frankly been rather embarrassed about the apparently paltry contribution of philosophy to knowledge compared to the multiple mansions of the disciplines of science. For the positivists, and by way of "solution," the previous wings of philosophy will be trimmed and the discipline brought down to earth to work, alongside its tutor, science, where it can, for once, be productive. This kind of overzealous and negative evaluation of traditional philosophy was not prepared to tolerate any pesky questions aloof from the ways and means of science in the march of knowledge. These thinkers stood prepared to divest philosophy of philosophy for the sake of knowledge. Oddly enough, for the positivists to be successful, their program would have meant in some debilitating manner, the end of philosophy.

For all of its shortcomings, and shortcomings there are, variant strains of postmodern philosophy may supply something that is needed in an age of science, over the objections of the logical positivists and more distanced in time, Francis Bacon. Postmodern candidates are by and large premodern contenders but in postmodernity they are revisiting the previously fenced conversation of modernity. With postmodernism there is a relaxing of commitment to rationality and science as the exclusive carriers of truth. This move was and still is disdainful to most modernists. Some thinkers, and paradoxically among them some repentant philosophers, are seen as undermining the traditional goal of thought and reflection in exalting such previously banished items as story, local narrative, poetry, and the nemesis of a presumed secured objectivity—particularity. Squeamishness over the character of the new inclusions, however, reflects the unsurrendered belief of modernity that modernity provides the best set of tools to achieve the goal. Such a view, moreover, usually reflects commitment to the rationalist obsession for the objectivity that feeds ravenous epistemological hunger. Postmodernism by contrast contends that modernity had the mistaken belief that a guarded epistemological diet was necessary to maintain objectivity. The ethos of modernism and the reigning rationalist tradition arose in the West by a suspicion of poetry, art, religion, or mythology—and with it images and feelings—in pursuit of the commendable goal of truth. Postmodernism appears ready and willing to overturn all or much of this previous work. Thus, one of the greatest paradoxes of Western thinking is in the recent mocking by the postmoderns of a modernity and modernists who thought that reason could fell any tree as long as the axe was sharp enough. Ironically, the builder and defender of modernity along with his axe may now find himself and his tools and methodologies toppled at the hands of the postmodernist. One wishes, however, that the ascending postmodernist will have decency enough to bury any of the felled in a civilized fashion while retaining and not obliterating the valuables of his predecessor. Equally important, one waits to see if the successor will build better worlds of thought than those he presumes to disparage.

CPSIA information can be obtained
at www.ICGtesting.com
Printed in the USA
LVOW04s1830161217
559937LV00002B/2/P